CROSSFIT FOR KIDS

CROSS✝FIT FOR KIDS

A PARENT'S GUIDE TO SPIRITUAL LEADERSHIP IN THE HOME

"Physical training is of some value,
but godliness has value for all things…"
I Timothy 4:8

JASON ANTHONY

CONTENTS

Dedicated to
all parents out there who are fighting for the
spiritual growth of their children.

INTRODUCTION

Not long ago I found myself at the Christian bookstore thumbing through several family devotional books. I was searching for a guide to assist me in taking my kids deeper in their journey with Jesus. I left the store frustrated at not being able to find one book that included more than a story topped off with two or three general questions at the end.

Don't get me wrong. Those were good for starters; but in my family, we were past scratching the surface and wanting to go deeper.

I shared my frustration with a long-time friend, ex-college roommate and great brother in Christ, Brian Pikalow. His response was, "Write your own devotionals!" Strangely, that thought had never crossed my mind. I always considered myself a speaker, not a writer. But I accepted the challenge, and what you hold in your hand is a project that took me more than two years to complete.

While writing CROSS FIT (which is for adults), and CROSS FIT FOR KIDS, I came across some interesting statistics that fueled my passion to help ordinary families like mine develop spiritually:

1. Less than 20% of parents with young children believe they are doing a good job of training their children morally and spiritually.

2. The same survey indicated that most children are biblically illiterate with only one-third believing the Bible is accurate in all of the principles it teaches.
   *Statistics taken from *Revolutionary Parenting* by George Barna.

Spiritually leading your kids can be challenging and flat-out frustrating at times. As a matter of fact, in my work as a professional speaker, I have discovered three main obstacles we parents face when attempting to spiritually lead our kids. These three obstacles include:

1. **Inadequacy:** Many parents feel inadequate sharing biblical truths with their children because they believe they lack the biblical knowledge to do so.
2. **Time:** Many parents do not feel they have ample time to prepare a quality devotion.
3. **Confidence:** Many parents lack the confidence to relate biblical truth to their children in a way they feel their children will enjoy and understand.

CROSS⸸FIT combined with CROSS⸸FIT FOR KIDS is a devotional series designed to remedy those three obstacles. Each chapter of both books contains the same Scripture, theme and title, but the devotionals are written on two different levels. The purpose of CROSS⸸FIT is to target the spiritual growth of you as a parent, and the purpose of CROSS⸸FIT FOR KIDS is to help you spiritually lead your children. The devotionals begin with Genesis and end in Revelation so that when completed, you and your family will have finished at least one devotion in each book of the Bible.

One publisher refused to publish this devotional because he said, "You are not spoon feeding the parents enough." As a parent, how does that make you feel? The spiritual growth of your children is too important merely to be spoon fed. Spiritual leadership in the home should be top priority for all us parents. Me spoon feeding you will only get you so far. It is time to go deeper with our families, in personal ways. So while this is a starting place, I encourage you to take it deeper and make it real for your family. I keep that letter pinned to my bulletin board for motivation.

So get ready... Get geared up... And let's deepen the journey together.

INSTRUCTIONS
TRUST ME. YOU NEED TO READ THESE BEFORE YOU START!

Newton's third law of motion states, *"For every action there is an equal and opposite reaction."* If there is ever an earthly law that applies in the spiritual realm, this is it! When I got serious about leading my kids into a deeper relationship with Jesus, the enemy got serious about attacking and distracting us. Mark my words, as you seek to train up your children in the Lord, the enemy will make equal attempts to pull your family in the opposite direction!

I know this is true. I'm living it with my four kids. The enemy will cause distractions (even using the kids as distractions). He will cause quarrels, discouragements and jealousy. And I don't mean disruptions over normal, everyday stuff. He will cause these disruptions concerning the Word of God.

This is especially true if you have more than one child. They will fight over who gets to the Bible verse first, who gets to pray first, who gets the right answer, so on and so forth.

No worries. Do not get discouraged. "For our struggle is not against flesh and blood, but ...against the powers of this dark world and against the spiritual forces of evil in the heavenly realms" (Ephesians 6:12). That is to say that our battle is not against one another, but against our enemy who is trying to disrupt, distract and discourage.

After several days of these types of distractions in our devotional time, I did a study on Ephesians 6:12 and helped my kids see who the battle is really against, and that it can be won by prayer. Hallelujah, we broke through!

If you hang in there and do regular devotions with your kids, you will find your devotional time getting smoother, flowing better, and becoming progressively more exciting as you see your kids flipping through the Word and understanding spiritual truths. Stay with it. Break through. It is so worth it.

GETTING THE MOST OUT OF YOUR
DEVOTIONAL TIME:

Preview the day's devotion before you lead your kids. In each devotion, I have included a visual idea to help your kids see and understand the written Word as you teach it. You will need to gather the visual objects yourself. Allow ample time to preview the devotion and gather the visuals.

In addition, there is a section in each devotion titled **Tie In**. In this section, I ask you to share a personal story/example from your life pertaining to the day's devotion. This is an important section! The **Tie In** allows your kids to hear your heart, experience your victories and defeats, and make the devotion more real to them. The **Tie In** section allows you to get vulnerable and real with your kids. Allow your mind ample time to think about the story/example you want to share with your kids.

Encourage your kids to talk, ask questions and make comments during the devotion **as long as** it pertains to the subject matter. Let them know this guideline up front and remind them as much as you need to so you stay on course.

Varying ages: If your kids vary in age, you will notice attention span differences. This can be very frustrating. My biggest challenge came with my six-year-old, Joshua. Sometimes he can handle five minutes and other times he can handle twenty-five minutes, but when he is done, he needs to be done. What do I do with my other three who want to keep going? I simply allow Joshua to excuse himself from the devotion when he feels he is done. He goes into another room and we keep the devotion going. I have noticed that as we are consistent with the devotions, Joshua can handle more and more.

Little bodies in motion: This is really interesting. My girl Haley can sit still indefinitely and talk about Scripture. Mike and Sam move around a little (from floor to couch or couch to floor) but they are tuned in. Josh, on the other hand, is the embodiment of perpetual motion! He's up, he's down, and he's upside down on his head. I found this to be irritating at first. I would force him to sit still and pay attention. What I discovered was that the more "still" I forced him to be, the less he was able to stay focused on the devotion. When I gave him the grace to move around, he tuned back in. Weird! He actually listens better while moving. So as long as he does not distract the other kids, I allow him to move around. Sometimes we give him something small and soft to squeeze. This helps him release his energy in a good way while participating in the devotion. Be full of grace. Adults sometimes try to pigeonhole kids. There is more than one way to learn, and if you have more than one kid, chances are each of them will learn in a different way. Go deep with your kids, but stay light hearted. What is more important: staying still or getting the message?

Personal Bible: I strongly recommend that each family member use his or her own Bible. If your kids don't own their own, take a family trip to the Christian bookstore and make a special time of it. Select a Bible translation that is in modern English such as the New International Version (NIV), New International Readers Version (NIRV), New Living Translation (NLT) or similar. Having their own Bibles adds a sense of importance, priority and ownership in studying God's Word.

Regardless of which translation you select, I recommend that everyone participating in the devotion use the same translation. This will cut down on confusion and make it easier for younger kids to follow along.

APPLICATION: Although I do include an **Application** of the devotion for your family, be as **intentional** and **creative** as you can about finding ways to apply the devotional to your children, specifically to their age and imagination levels. Think about elementary school, lunch room, recess, P.E. class, their friends etc. For example, Mark Chapter 10 talks about blind Bartimaeus who called out to Jesus for mercy. As the kids and I talked about the meaning of mercy, I asked, "How can you show mercy to others?" Joshua told how he purposely slowed down while playing tag at recess because a certain boy was too slow to catch anybody and he was getting discouraged. The other kids kept tagging this one boy because they knew he wouldn't be able to catch them again. Josh showed him mercy by slowing down and letting himself get caught. He got the lesson! At six years old, that's mercy.

Keep your spiritual antennae up by looking for points of application throughout your day that tie back into a recent devotion. Then talk to your kids about them. While you're at the store, in the car, or eating dinner with your kids, look for life examples to reinforce what you've recently discussed.

Encourage, encourage, encourage! Try not to talk down to your kids, but look for ways to encourage them at every turn not only during the devotion, but in their journey of life.

Location: Be comfortable and casual. Sit on the couch or floor or both. If you have an area outside, utilize that space from time to time. If you are taking a family trip, do your devotion in the hotel room or out on the pool deck. We love doing this because it adds variety and builds memories in different places.

Begin with the basics: Begin by familiarizing your children with the Bible. Show them simple facts such as:

1. The Bible is divided into two sections: the Old Testament and the New Testament.
2. The Old Testament is before the birth of Jesus and the New Testament is from the birth of Jesus on.
3. The Bible is made up of sixty-six different books

SPICE IT UP:

These are fun games you can frequently play with your kids.

Sword Drill: This is a game I play with my kids to help them find books of the Bible, chapters and finally verses. Call out the name of a book, Matthew for example, and have them try to find it as quickly as possible. I will give them hints as needed. **Note: It may not be a good idea to have your kids race each other as this could lead to discouragement for the one who is slowest.** Instead, tell your kids they are racing themselves, and in that way they at least always get to the book they are looking for. After several weeks, add a chapter along with the book. Turn to Matthew 11 for example. When they get good at that process, start calling out a book, chapter and verse. As your kids get used to the game, it's also fun to have them take turns at calling out their own books, chapters and verses.

Book Quiz: This is another game I play to help my kids familiarize themselves with the Bible. Beginning in either the Old Testament or the New Testament, have the kids name as many books of the Bible in a row as they can. When we first started, my kids did not know that Genesis was the first book of the Old Testament. **Variation:** If you have more than one child, you can have them rotate naming the books in order. For example, one child starts with Matthew. The next child says Mark, etc. **Note:** I set a rule that my wife and I are the only ones who can help or give hints. This helped my kids not feel discouraged just because they might not have known the next book.

The teachers at my kid's school have them memorize ten to twenty new spelling words every week. In that vein, memorizing sixty-six books is not an impossible task. Both are important, but only one has eternal significance.

Scripture memory: Every week, choose a Scripture to memorize. I usually, but not always, choose a verse out of Monday or Tuesday's devotion. It increases the devotion's application, and choosing one early in the week gives us more time to memorize it. I type the verses on a sheet of paper and keep them on the refrigerator. **Note: Scripture memory is essential to your kids' spiritual growth because recalling the Scripture during teachable moments brings instant application to the Word of God in their lives.** For example, I Timothy 6:18 is a verse on sharing we've memorized. As you know, people in general, but kids especially, struggle in the area of generosity. When my kids are not sharing or being generous, all I need to do is ask them what I Timothy 6:18 says. If memorizing a Scripture per week is too much, then try two a month.

Bible trivia: This is a fun activity that helps reinforce what your kids are learning spiritually. The beauty of this game is that it can be played anytime, anywhere and no materials are needed. Whether you are walking down the street, driving in the car, playing in the yard or traveling, you can play this game with your kids. Simply ask them questions about past devotions you've done together. Ask them questions about Bible characters. Ask them to name the first five books of the Old Testament, or to name the gospels. Ask them to quote Scripture they've been memorizing. Ask them details about parables or stories you've been reading through. **Note: Be patient and give them time to formulate an answer. Give them hints or clues if needed. Encourage them all the way.**

Last, do not feel you have to cover each devotion in one day. You may choose to stay on the Genesis devotion for two or three

days. That's fine. Do not allow the enemy to make you feel guilty for missing a day. I'll tell you right now, you will miss days. That's okay. The goal is consistency.

Note: There are places in the text where I will ask direct questions, and provide the answers in parenthesis. The goal is to get your kids to answer the questions directly, but the answers are provided to you just in case.

CROSS✝FIT FOR KIDS

IT'S IN THE PACKAGING

GENESIS 3:1-7

OBJECTIVE: To help your children discover that Satan's plan is to trick them into not trusting God.

VISUALS: Fake snake, beautifully wrapped gift box and an ugly wrapped gift box. Put money or candy in the ugly box before you wrap it.

WARM UP: Pray. Read Genesis 3:1-7 with your children and discuss the following:

1. Reread verse 1 together. Ask: Who does the serpent represent? (Satan - which literally means adversary or enemy.) Satan is your enemy who continually tries to get you not to trust God.
2. Ask: What do you picture when you think of a serpent? **Visual:** Use your fake snake here. Ask: Why weren't Adam and Eve scared of the serpent? Help your children discover that the serpent was not cursed to crawl on its belly until verse 14 which was after He tricked Adam and Eve. Since the serpent was created as an angel, He was quite beautiful before He was cursed.
3. Ask and explain: Why do you think God told Adam and Eve not to eat from the tree in the middle of the garden? God was not being mean, but rather He was trying to protect Adam and Eve. If they ate from the tree in the middle, the tree of the "knowledge of good and evil,"

God knew sin would enter their lives and they would die (Genesis 2:16,17). Explain that God's commands are for their protection, and ultimately for their blessing. Help your kids see that Satan's goal is to trick and fool them into not trusting God and His Word.

4. Explain the following: In verse 6, Satan showed Adam and Eve how good, pleasing and desirable the tree was to tempt them not to trust in what God said. Satan's main weapon against you is trickery. He tries to get you to believe that sin is good, pleasing and desirable, but sin always leads to sadness and disappointment. Just because something looks beautiful or a situation seems right does not mean it is God's will. Pray and talk to God about everything and wait to hear from Him before you make a decision. You can always ask Mom or Dad for help.

KEY POINT: Trust God and His Word.

APPLICATION: Display the wrapped boxes in front of your children, but don't have anyone open them yet. Have the children look at the boxes. Ask them which one they would rather open. Ask them how they would feel if you told them they should not open the beautiful one, because it would lead to disappointment. Have your children then open each of the boxes and discuss how they felt when they discovered the contents. Mention how Satan packages sin beautifully to try to trick them. Often what is really valuable (the blessings of God) are packaged in a way that you would not expect.

TIE IN: Share with your children a time of victory when you trusted God in a situation, or a time when you failed to trust God.

PRAY TOGETHER

THE PASSOVER

EXODUS 12:1-13

OBJECTIVE: To help your children discover the seriousness of sin and the incredible grace of God.

VISUALS: A toy stuffed lamb and your front door. If the weather is bad, do this inside.

WARM UP: Read Exodus 12:1-13 with your children and discuss the following:

1. Place the stuffed lamb in front of your children and, in your own words, recreate the Passover account for them. Let them know that the death of the firstborn was the last plague before the people were set free. Go out by your front door and show them the door frame where you would have had to place the lamb's blood on behalf of your family, Then read verse 13 to your children. Explain to them that it was because of the lamb's blood that God's judgment passed over the people and forgave them.
2. Ask and explain: How do you feel about the innocent lamb that had to be killed for the people's sin? If you were the firstborn boy in Egypt, how would you have felt about the Passover lamb? Remember, either the lamb or the firstborn boy would die because sin had to be judged.
3. Explain to your children that although the Passover occurred fifteen hundred years before

Jesus' birth, the Passover was a picture of what Jesus would do for us. Jesus is called the "Lamb of God" (John 1:29). Mention the following: Jesus, as the Lamb of God, allowed Himself to be sacrificed on a cross so that by believing in Him you would receive forgiveness and the judgment for your sin would be passed over. As you believe in Jesus Christ, the blood is applied to your life. Just as the blood of the lamb needed to be applied to the doorpost of the Israelites' homes, the blood of Christ needs to be applied to the door of your heart for forgiveness.

4. Mention: The blood of the Savior is applied to you for salvation when you trust that Jesus was the lamb who died so you can be forgiven. When you ask Him into your life as Savior and Lord, His shed blood applies to the door of your heart and you are forgiven and saved.

KEY POINT: Jesus is your Passover Lamb.

APPLICATION: This is a wonderful opportunity to lead your child/children to Christ if they have never confessed Jesus as Lord and Savior. Take this time to pray through that decision with them: "Jesus, thank you for loving me enough to die on the cross for my sins. I know that your blood was shed for me. Right now by faith, I open the door of my heart and ask you to come in and be my Lord and Savior. Thank you for your forgiveness and grace. Help me to live to glorify you. Amen."

PRAY TOGETHER

STRANGE FIRE

LEVITICUS 9:23-10:2

OBJECTIVE: To encourage your kids to rely on God and not their own abilities.

VISUALS: A candle and matches or a lighter.

WARM UP: Read Leviticus 9:23-10:2 with your children and discuss the following:

1. Explain that a censer was like a pot which was used for carrying fire for burnt offerings. Burnt offerings were provided for the forgiveness of sins and consisted of an animal being killed and placed on the altar. As a sign that God accepted the offering, the animal would be consumed by fire from God. The fire used in these censers was to be taken from that altar. If your children think that is cruel or mean, use it as a time to stress the ugliness and seriousness of sin.

2. Ask and explain: What did Nadab and Abihu do to make God angry? **Visual:** Light the candle as a representation of a burnt offering to the Lord. Next, light a match or use your lighter to show how Nadab and Abihu tried to add to the Lord's fire. When the people celebrated their forgiveness by the altar, Nadab and Abihu saw it as an opportunity to become famous with the people by adding their own fire. This showed great disre-

spect for God in front of all the people, so God made an example of them.

3. Ask your kids to pretend they are on a sports team and their coach calls out the play. Instead, they decide to add to the play by doing their own thing. Ask: How do you think the coach would respond? Could your actions hurt your team? How? By not being obedient to your coach, what are you telling him/her?

4. Mention the following: God is your head coach in life and He has certain "plays" He wants you to follow for your own good. The Ten Commandments in Exodus 20 are a great example. What if you said, "I don't need God's direction. I can figure out life on my own." Will God honor that? (No. He's not literally going to consume you with fire, but He won't bless your life either. God wants us to rely on Him. He can accomplish far more through us than we ever can do on our own).

KEY POINT: Strange fire is saying you don't need God in your life.

APPLICATION: This week, ask your children to focus on their need for God in the things they are trying to accomplish. Some examples might include: homework, a test, obedience to parents, cleaning their room, helping around the house. Instead of trying to do life on their own, encourage your children to continually ask God to help them. Express why this is a great habit to build in life, because it will bring about blessing rather than curse.

TIE IN: Tell your kids about a time when either you didn't listen to God in a situation or a time when you did. What was the result.

PRAY TOGETHER

WALKING IN HUMILITY

NUMBERS 14:1-11

OBJECTIVE: To help your children see the importance of humility in their walk with God.

VISUALS: An old tee-shirt that you can tear. Tear it when you talk about Joshua and Caleb tearing their clothes.

WARM UP: Read Numbers 14:1-11 with your children and discuss the following:

1. Explain that twelve spies went to explore the Promised Land. Two came back with a good report because they had strong faith and ten came back with a bad report because they had weak faith. Read verses 1-4 again. Ask: What is the result of having weak faith? Help your children see that as a result of weak faith, the people whined, wept and complained.

2. Ask: What was Moses' and Aaron's response to the people whining and weeping? Read verse 5 again. Explain how Moses and Aaron fell face down. This means they bowed down and prayed for God to help them. Moses and Aaron in fact often "fell face down" to pray because they needed God's help. Emphasize how asking God for help shows humility. Mention that humility means realizing you need God's help instead of trying to solve problems on your own.

3. Point out that although Joshua and Caleb were

good leaders, instead of showing humility, they tried to solve their problems on their own by yelling at the Israelites. See verses 6-9. Explain to your children that when people tore their clothes in the Bible, it was often done in anger, frustration and disbelief of the situation taking place. Ask: Have you ever tried to resolve a conflict with angry words? What happened?

4. Explain that shouting matches never work to solve conflict and God does not respond to this kind of anger. Ask and explain: What did the Israelites want to do to Joshua and Caleb in response to their anger? See verse 10. Help your children understand that angry words are no way to resolve conflict. God did respond to Moses' and Aaron's humility. He in fact spoke to Moses and Aaron because of their humility. God honors humility because it becomes the open door through which He is able to work in that person to bring about His plans.

KEY POINT: God works mightily in your life when you show humility.

APPLICATION: Ask your kids to notice the next time they are in a conflict with another person, and to stop and pray. Have them ask God for help and wisdom in solving the conflict.

TIE IN: Share with your kids about a time when you went to the Lord in humility and asked for His help.

PRAY TOGETHER

REMEMBERING GOD

Chapter 5

DEUTERONOMY 8:1-5 AND VERSE 11

OBJECTIVE: To help your children see that God wants them to obey Him so He can bless them.

VISUALS: Some items that are of high quality and some items that are bad or rotten. For example, you may choose some good food or fruit along with some that is moldy or spoiled. Or display some nice clothes along with some old, worn, ratty ones, etc.

WARM UP: Pray. Read Deuteronomy 8:1-5 and verse 11 with your children and discuss the following:

1. Explain to your children the difference between a conditional promise and an unconditional promise. A conditional promise means certain criteria must be met in order for the promise to be fulfilled and unconditional promise means the promise will be fulfilled regardless of your actions. For example, you may promise to take your children to the park if they clean their rooms. Or, as an unconditional promise, you may promise to love your children no matter what.

2. Confirm that God's love is unconditional. There is nothing your kids can do to earn it. However, explain that His blessings come with conditions. For example, "Children, obey your parents in the Lord, for this is right. Honor your father and mother – which is the first commandment with

a promise – that it may go well with you and that you may enjoy long life on the earth" (Ephesians 6:1-3). Tell your children that if they obey Mom and Dad, God will bless them.

3. According to verse 11, what is a sign that you are forgetting about the Lord in your life? Help your children see that when they fail to observe or obey the Lord's commands, they are forgetting about the Lord.

4. Display the good and bad items in front of your kids. Emphasize the fact that as they are obedient to God throughout their lives, God will bless them. He will bless them not only with food, clothes and other physical needs, but spiritually. It's when people forget about the Lord and fail to follow Him that blessings fade.

KEY POINT: God will bless your life as you walk in obedience with Him.

APPLICATION: Ask and request: Is there an area of your life in which God wants you to be more obedient? What is it? Before you end the devotion, pray about that area and commit it to God.

TIE IN: Tell your children about a time when you were obedient to God and God blessed you for it.

PRAY TOGETHER

ACHAN'S SIN

JOSHUA 7:1-6, 10-12, 19-26

OBJECTIVE: To help your children see that sin affects everyone in the house.

VISUALS: Articles of gold and silver if you have any. Otherwise, just use plain, old money! In addition, some cord or rope that you can unravel to separate the strings.

WARM UP: Pray. Read Joshua 7:1-6, 10-12, 19-26, with your children and discuss the following:

1. Explain to your kids that many times God allowed the Israelites to plunder or take the riches of the city they had just conquered. Jericho was different. Read Joshua 6:18,19. God wanted the Israelites to devote all the riches to God as a sacrifice to honor Him for the victory at Jericho. Did all the Israelites obey? No, Achan kept some for himself. As you explain this to your children, have the gold, silver or money laid out in front of them.

2. Ask your kids, "Did Achan's sin affect only him or did his sin affect others? Who did it affect?" Explain how it affected the whole Israelite community. Share with them that because of Achan's sin, God's favor was gone from the people. As a result, fathers and husbands died in battle. The Bible says, "The hearts of the people melted and became like water." Because of Achan's sin,

the people knew that God's power and favor had left them, and they became afraid. Achan's whole family had to die because of his sin.

3. Ask your kids if when they sin, does it affect only them or does it affect everybody in the house? Explain how it affects everybody in the house. How? When one person sins, it disrupts God's peace, joy and blessing in the house. Sin brings arguments and discord. Bring out your cord as a visual. Explain that if the cords remain wrapped together, the rope is strong. Sin causes discord. Begin to unravel the cord as a visual. Now the rope is weaker and separated. Sin weakens relationships and separates us from each other and God. Forgiveness brings restoration.

KEY POINT: Everyone in the house is affected when one person sins.

APPLICATION: Mention how God's favor and blessing were not going to return to His people until the items that Achan stole were removed from among them. Ask: Do you have any items (music, movies, books, magazines, types of trading cards, certain toys, clothes, etc.) that you don't think God wants you to keep? Ask Him to let you know. If God points something out to you, will you remove it from your house?

TIE IN: Tell your children about a time when God led you to "clean house," to remove an item or two that you knew did not honor Him.

PRAY TOGETHER

REAPING WHAT YOU HAVE SOWN

JUDGES 1:1-7

OBJECTIVE: To help your children understand the principle of sowing and reaping.

VISUALS: A fork, a spoon, a cup without a handle.

WARM UP: Pray. Read Judges 1:1-7 with your children and discuss the following:

1. Have your children tuck their thumbs into their palms and try to pick up a set of silverware and a cup without a handle. Discuss how that feels. Have them try to walk on the outer edge of their feet without using their big toes. Give them time to talk about how that feels.

2. Ask them what happened to Adoni-Bezek. (He had his thumbs and toes cut off.) Ask your children if they think that was fair. Why or why not? Explain to your children that Adoni-Bezek reaped what he had sown to seventy other kings. How you treat others will often come back to you, whether good or bad. Stress to your children the golden rule: Do unto others as you would have them do unto you.

3. Explain how the principle of sowing and reaping applies to every area of life. For example, if your kids were on a sports team and did not go to practice very often or did not give it their all while practicing, how do they think they would play?

The same can be said for taking a test. If they pay attention in class and study, they will do much better on the test. If they sow good study habits, they will reap good test results. Ask: What other examples of sowing and reaping can you think of? Try to get them to think of both positive and negative examples.

4. Ask and explain: How does the principle of sowing and reaping apply to your spiritual life? Help your children understand that as they sow into their own lives by reading God's Word, developing their prayer life and worshipping God regularly, they will sense God's presence in their lives more and more. God will begin to use them mightily for His Kingdom and they will have a definite sense of purpose for their lives.

KEY POINT: In life, what you sow is what you will reap.

APPLICATION: Ask the following: How has the principle of reaping and sowing been true in your life? Think of areas of your life in which you need to sow more carefully in order to reap results that will be more honoring to God. Pray through those as you end today's devotion.

TIE IN: Share with your children a time in your life when you reaped what you sowed – whether good or bad.

PRAY TOGETHER

KINSMAN REDEEMER

RUTH 2:19, 20

OBJECTIVE: To help your children understand what the term kinsman redeemer means and how it relates to their relationship with Jesus Christ.

VISUALS: Your child's prized possession.

WARM UP: Pray. Read Ruth 2:19, 20 with your children and discuss the following:

1. Explain to your children that the book of Ruth is a story about a kinsman redeemer. Kinsman means family member and to redeem means to regain possession of something that was once lost.

2. Explain how in the book of Ruth, a woman named Naomi had a husband who died. Naomi's two sons had also died. Naomi was left with her two daughters-in-law, Orpah and Ruth. Orpah left to go back to her hometown, but Ruth promised to stay with Naomi. Together, Ruth and Naomi traveled to Bethlehem where Naomi was from. Ruth and Naomi had nothing left: no family, no money, and no place to live. In Bethlehem, they met a good man named Boaz. Boaz turned out to be a close relative, a kinsman of theirs, and he wanted to help them. Boaz redeemed Ruth and Naomi by marrying Ruth. When Boaz married Ruth, Ruth and Naomi were officially brought

Cross Fit FOR KIDS

back into the family again and received all the blessings therein: family, provision for all their needs, and a place to live. Boaz was their kinsman redeemer.

3.   Hold up your child's prized possession. Share with your kids this hypothetical example by asking: What if your prized possession was accidentally sold in the family garage sale? How would you feel? Would you want to get it back? Tell your child, "I think I know who bought it. I will go to his house, explain what happened and buy it back." Explain that you have acted as Boaz, the kinsman redeemer, when you regained possession of something that was lost.

4.   Explain how Boaz is a picture of Jesus Christ. Jesus Christ is the ultimate Kinsman Redeemer. Mention: God created you in His image. He created you to know Him, but your sin has separated you from God. Jesus Christ willingly went to the cross, was crucified and buried, and on the third day rose again so that your sins would be forgiven and you would be brought back into His family. By believing in Jesus Christ, He becomes your personal Kinsman Redeemer.

KEY POINT: Jesus Christ is your Kinsman Redeemer.

APPLICATION: What are some ways to thank Jesus for being your Kinsman Redeemer?

TIE IN: Share with your children the day you accepted Jesus as your Kinsman Redeemer.

PRAY TOGETHER

FACING GIANTS

I SAMUEL 17:1-11 AND 32-50

OBJECTIVE: To help your children have faith in God when facing "giants" in their lives.

9

VISUALS: An object weighing roughly sixteen pounds, a large action figure to represent Goliath, and a small action figure to represent David. You can also use yourself and your child as the action figures.

WARM UP: Pray. Read I Samuel 17:1-11 and 32-50 with your children and discuss the following:

1. Explain to your children that there is a battle getting ready to take place between the Philistine army, who did not believe in God, and the Israelite army, who did believe in God. The Philistines were on one hill and the Israelites on another, with a valley between them: picture an athletic stadium setting. Show the children the action figures and let them visualize how big Goliath was compared to David. Goliath was nine feet tall, fully armored and undefeated in battle. Let your children hold the sixteen pound object. Explain that this was the weight (six hundred shekels) of just the iron tip of Goliath's spear.

2. Mention how in what was probably his early teen years, David is described as "only a boy" (verse 33). David was old enough to take care of his father's sheep, but not old enough to serve in

an army. Unlike the undefeated champion, David had no
battle experience. Goliath challenged the Israelites to send
out a man to fight one on one in a "winner takes all match."
The losers would have to serve the winners. David, full of
faith, accepted the challenge!

3. Explain that in life, giants are often more than or something
    different than just big people. "Giants" can be difficult situ-
    ations you face, hard decisions you must make, choosing to
    do what's right no matter what others think, etc. Ask and
    explain: What are some of the hardest choices or situations
    you had to face so far in life? Read verses 45 and 47. What
    can you learn from David about how to face "giants" in
    your life? Explain that David knew in his heart that God
    was bigger than Goliath. David knew that through faith,
    God could use him to gain victory over Goliath. God used
    David just the way he was, as a boy.

KEY POINT: Through faith, God will see you through any "giant" situation in life.

APPLICATION: Ask: What "giant" situation are you facing now? Explain
that as David said, "The battle is the Lord's." Ask your kids to
pray that God give them strength and victory over that giant.

TIE IN: Share with your children a time when you faced a "giant" situation in your life and how the Lord proved faithful during that
time.

PRAY TOGETHER

THE CRIPPLED ONE

II SAMUEL 9

OBJECTIVE: To help your children identify with being "crippled" spiritually and to experience God's grace in the midst of being crippled.

VISUALS: A blindfold, a crutch or cane if you have one, something to tie a hand behind the back, and a piece of wide masking tape to put (gently!) over a mouth.

WARM UP: Pray. Read II Samuel 9 with your children and discuss the following:

1. Use the visuals to help your children experience what it might be like to live with a physical limitation. Give your children specific tasks while having one or more limitations. For example, have them try to communicate to you with a piece of tape over their mouths or tie their shoes with one hand behind their backs, etc. Ask them, "What does it mean to be crippled?"

2. Ask and explain: In what way was Mephibosheth crippled? How did he get that way? See II Samuel 4:4 for the answer. After King Saul died along with his son Jonathon, King David was the new king. In that time period, whenever a new king came into power, he would generally wipe out all of the previous king's family because they were considered a threat to the new king. Fearing that David may have Mephibosheth killed, the nurse

Chapter

10

Cross Fit FOR KIDS

41

rushed to escape and accidentally dropped Mephibosheth, which crippled his feet.

3. Ask and explain: How did King David treat Mephibosheth? He was invited to sit at the King's table which meant incredible blessing and provision. Who do you think King David represents in this story and why? He represents God the Father because he showed great kindness and grace to Mephibosheth. Who do you think Mephibosheth represented in this story and why? He represents us. We are crippled spiritually because of our sin.

4. Ask and explain: Did Mephibosheth have to fix his crippled feet before he sat at David's table? No, he could not fix his feet. Do you have to fix your spiritually crippled condition before you are able to fellowship with God? No, you can't fix your sin. Through God's grace, you are forgiven and accepted by God the way you are, just as David accepted Mephibosheth.

KEY POINT: God loves you and accepts you the way you are.

APPLICATION: Ask your kids to continually enjoy God's mercy and blessing by "going to His table" and confessing your sin. At the end of this devotion, encourage your kids to spend a few moments with God and ask Him if there is any unconfessed sin in their lives. Encourage them to confess as God directs.

TIE IN: Share about a time when you sensed God's love despite a failure you experienced.

PRAY TOGETHER

A RIGHTEOUS REQUEST

I KINGS 3:5-15

OBJECTIVE: To help your children seek the heart of God.

VISUALS: A stack of money (even if it's Monopoly money), magazine pictures of objects your children love (video games, certain toys, hobbies, etc.), a Bible.

WARM UP: Pray. Read I Kings 3:5-15 with your children and discuss the following:

1. Ask your children, "If you could have three wishes, what would you wish for?" Lay out the visuals on the floor or table and, after prompting your children to be as honest as they can be, ask them if they had to choose just one of the items laid out, which would they choose and why? Be accepting and patient with their answers.

2. Ask and explain: What was the one thing Solomon asked God for? Why do you think Solomon asked God for wisdom? Do you think Solomon wanted to ask God for other things? What might some of those things have been? Why was God so pleased that Solomon asked for wisdom to lead His people? God's heart was with the people of Israel and He loved them very much.

3. Ask and explain: Why is it important for you to have godly wisdom in your life? His wisdom guides you to make choices that will honor and glorify God every day. What are some ways God

reveals His wisdom to us? He reveals Himself through His Word, Holy Spirit, through godly people in our lives.

4. Ask and explain: What was Solomon doing just before God spoke to him? (Worshipping.) God speaks to you through His Holy Spirit when you worship. Worship puts your heart in touch with God's heart. Reading the Word of God allows you to hear the heart of God. When you are in touch with the heart of God, you ask God for the right things. Your prayers honor Him and He honors your prayers.

KEY POINT: When you are in touch with the heart of God, you ask God for the right things.

APPLICATION: Read James 1:5. Ask: What does this verse say about asking God for wisdom? Have your children talk about some areas of their lives in which they need God's help and wisdom. Specifically pray for those areas as a family and check up on those areas frequently.

TIE IN: Tell about a time in your life when you really needed God's help and wisdom. Explain how God met your need.

PRAY TOGETHER

YOU ARE NOT ALONE

II KINGS 6: 15-17

12

OBJECTIVE: To help your children understand that God is always with them and ready to help them in every situation.

VISUALS: A blindfold.

WARM UP: Pray. Read II Kings 6: 15-17 with your children and discuss the following:

1. Place the blindfold around your children's heads so that they cannot see. Have them listen to your verbal instructions as you safely guide them through part of your house. For example: Take three steps forward... Turn to the right... Take five steps forward... Turn left. The purpose of this exercise is to show your children that though they cannot see you, you are still there to help safely guide them. In the same way, though you cannot see God, He is always with you to help guide you through life.

2. Explain Elisha's situation to your children: an evil king was chasing him because of his faith in God. The evil king and his army surrounded Elisha and his servant in the town of Dothan. Elisha's servant panicked, but Elisha sized up the situation and said, "Don't be afraid. Those who are with us are more than those who are with them" (verse 16). Ask: What do you think Elisha meant

Cross Fit FOR KIDS

when he said, "Those who are with us are more than those who are with them?"

3. Mention: God is with you all the time. Explain to your children that in life they will face tough times and challenging situations. When they are faced with these tough times, they can either respond like Elisha or like Elisha's servant. What was the difference in the way Elisha responded from the way his servant responded?

KEY POINT: God is always with you in every situation to help you. As you are obedient to God's commands, you will be able to sense His presence in your life in greater ways.

APPLICATION: Explain how the first thing Elisha did when his servant called him outside to look at the army surrounding them was to pray. He prayed that God would open the eyes of his servant so that his servant could see that God was with them. Tell your kids that the next time they find themselves in tough situations, they should pray for God to help them. Have them report back to you (Mom or Dad).

TIE IN: Tell your children of a tough situation you went through. In what way did you sense the presence of the Lord? How did that affect your faith?

PRAY TOGETHER

BROADER BOUNDARIES

I CHRONICLES 4:9,10

OBJECTIVE: To help your children see that it is okay to ask for God's blessing when they ask with the right motives.

WARM UP: Pray. Read I Chronicles 4:9,10 with your children and discuss the following:

1. Ask: Do you think Jabez was being selfish in his prayer? Why or why not?
2. Ask and explain: Is it wrong to ask God to bless you? No, not if you pray with a pure heart and an unselfish attitude. God wants to bless you. Psalm 84:11 reads, "For the Lord God is a sun and shield; the Lord bestows favor and honor; **no good thing does he withhold from those whose walk is blameless**." If you pray that others would like you so you could be popular, that you would have nice things so you could show off in front of others, or that you would be made strong so you can put others down, God will not honor those sorts of prayers because they are selfish. On the other hand, if you pray for guidance to serve God's will, you will be blessed.
3. Explain that verse 9 reads, "Jabez was more honorable than his brothers." Jabez was a man who loved and honored God. He was head and shoulders above his brothers in devotion to God.

Jabez had a pure heart. Explore the four parts of Jabez's prayer by reading the following and explaining:

1. "Oh, that you would bless me..." As you live for the Lord and are faithful to follow Him, you will make choices and partake in activities that glorify God. I Samuel 2:30 reads, "Those who honor me, I will honor." You will be blessed and feel blessed as you honor God.

2. "...and enlarge my territory!" This would be like you praying for God to increase the number of people who know you and respect you. Why? So that your walk with the Lord will encourage them also to want to walk with the Lord. Not so that you will become popular, but so that the Lord Jesus Christ would become popular with those who know you.

3. "Let your hand be with me..." As God blesses you and enlarges your territory, you will have greater influence on others and a greater temptation to get prideful, to think of yourself more highly than you ought (Romans 12:3). You will need God's hand, His power in your life to keep you pure and humble.

4. "...and keep me from harm so that I will be free from pain." Jabez is praying that God keep him from evil. Sin causes pain in your life and in the lives of others around you. Jabez is selflessly praying that God keeps him from causing pain in other people's lives.

KEY POINT: God is ready and willing to bless those who pray with a pure heart.

APPLICATION: Using the four parts above, pray each part out loud over your children as you close the devotion.

PRAY TOGETHER

A LIFE FOR GOD

II CHRONICLES 7:12-18

OBJECTIVE: To inspire your children to live wholeheartedly for the Lord.

VISUALS: A game of follow the leader, and some prizes. The prizes are not meant to be theirs to keep necessarily, but rather an illustration of God's blessing in the game.

WARM UP: Pray. Read II Chronicles 7:12-18 with your children and discuss the following:

1. Mention that verse 14 begins with, "…if my people." Ask: Who are God's people? Point out to your children that the Bible teaches that when they believe in Jesus, God adopts them into His family forever. By faith in Jesus, they are now children of God and considered "His people."

2. Explain that in the Old Testament, the Israelites were considered God's chosen people. However, the Israelites, from the time they left Egypt, seesawed in their faith. Like a seesaw going up and down, the Israelites had times of great faith which brought blessings, and times of disobedience during which they suffered the consequences. God sent prophets to warn them of their wicked ways. When the Israelites ignored the prophets, God sent hard times, disasters, plagues, etc., to get them to turn back. Jeremiah the prophet warned

the Israelites for forty years to repent and turn back to the Lord, but they never listened. As a result, God allowed King Nebuchadnezzar of Babylon to destroy Jerusalem and take them into captivity. Mention: It is never God's heart to use hard times to bring you back to Him. His heart is that you would never seesaw in your faith in the first place.

3. Explain that verse 14 gives four great points to live a life for God. 1. *Humble yourself:* know that you need God's help to follow Him. 2. *Pray:* express your need for God's help through prayer. 3. *Seek His face:* look to find what God wants for your life and listen to His voice. 4. *Turn from your wicked ways:* be quick to admit to God when you've made a mistake, confess it and make the situation right.

KEY POINT: A person living for God is one who is obedient to His Word.

APPLICATION: Play two rounds of follow the leader. Tell the children to follow you wherever you go in the house, but have them occasionally deliberately disobey you by turning away. In the second round, have them follow you faithfully and reward them with whatever you chose in the "visuals" section. Let them know that God will bless them for their obedience. It is also important for your children to understand that God's blessings will not always be physical (money, things, etc.), but sometimes spiritual (joy, peace, confidence, love, etc.).

TIE IN: Share with your children a time when God used someone or circumstances to refocus your faith.

PRAY TOGETHER

COMPLETE THE WORK

EZRA 4 – 6:12

OBJECTIVE: To help your children see that they will face opposition as they follow the Lord, but God's will always prevails.

VISUALS: Building blocks, Lego's, Lincoln Logs, a deck of cards – anything that you can use to make a mini building. The cards would be for a card house if you did not have blocks or Lego's.

WARM UP: Pray. Read Ezra 4-6:12 with your children. If you feel this passage of Scripture is too lengthy for your children, familiarize yourself with it beforehand and share only portions. Discuss the following:

1. Explain the current events in this Scripture: God had allowed King Nebuchadnezzar of Babylon to destroy Jerusalem and carry the Israelites into captivity for seventy years. Jeremiah the prophet warned them to repent, but the Israelites stubbornly refused. At the end of the seventy years of captivity, King Cyrus of Persia conquered Babylon and ruled the land. Zerubbabel, a good, godly man received permission from King Cyrus to go back with some of the Jewish people to rebuild the temple and restore worship in Jerusalem.

2. Have your children construct a building out of the materials listed in the visuals. The building will represent a mini model of the temple that the

Israelites would have used to worship God. Join them in the construction, but unbeknownst to them, play the part of the enemy. Put pieces where they don't belong. When they catch on to what you are doing, change your tactics. Take blocks off that they have put on, hide blocks and use discouraging words to try and get them to stop building. Help your children see that this was the same tactic the enemies of the Jews used. In verses 1-3, the enemies tried to join the Israelites to ruin the work from the inside. When that did not work, the enemy tried to spread discouragement and fear (verses 4 and 5). When that did not work, the enemy wrote letters to the kings to get the building of the temple to stop.

KEY POINT: God wants to use you to finish His work here on earth. You will face opposition or spiritual warfare when you are doing His work, so be prepared for challenges; but know that blessing will come if you don't quit.

APPLICATION: Remind the children that "work" that God wants them to do may be in the form of telling a classmate about Jesus, reaching out in kindness to a person who is not well liked, asking forgiveness if they wronged someone, telling the truth, completing a project or task that God has put on their heart, etc. Ask them: Is there any "work" that God has put on your heart that you need to finish?

TIE IN: Tell about a time when you were obedient to a task God was calling you to. What opposition did you face and how did it affect you?

PRAY TOGETHER

GOD STIRS THE HEART

NEHEMIAH 1:1-4 AND 2:4, 5

OBJECTIVE: To challenge your children to respond to God's calling in the right way.

VISUALS: Blocks, Lego's, Lincoln Logs or materials your children can build a wall with.

WARM UP: Pray. Read Nehemiah 1:1-4 and 2:4, 5 with your children and discuss the following:

1. Ask: According to these verses, what did God put in Nehemiah's heart to do? Could God have chosen another person to complete that task? Was Nehemiah obedient to what God wanted him to do?

2. Read Ephesians 6:1-3 with your children. Ask and explain: According to verse 1, what has God called you to do? When I ask you to clean your room or pull weeds or help with the dishes, do you ever wish someone else would complete that task? Just like God chose Nehemiah to rebuild the wall, He chose you for the special task of obeying your parents. Did God choose Nehemiah to rebuild the wall to make Nehemiah's life extra hard? No, God gave Nehemiah the task of building the wall because He wanted to bless Nehemiah. In the same way, God does not give you the command of obeying your parents because He wants you to

be miserable, but because He wants to bless you. Emphasize Ephesians 6:3.

3. Mention how Nehemiah did not whine, complain or become angry at the task to which God had called him. Instead, Nehemiah was eager and willing to serve and obey God. Nehemiah knew that to be called by God was a very special thing. So not only was Nehemiah obedient to what God called him to do, but he did it in the right way. Obedience is great, but to be obedient with a joyful heart, a willing spirit, and a good attitude, is the kind of obedience with which God is pleased.

KEY POINT: Willing obedience with a glad heart brings great blessing.

APPLICATION: Give your children a task to complete (clean their room or part of the house, pull weeds, etc.). Challenge your children to complete the task with a joyful heart. After the task is complete, look at the work with them and ask them how it feels to have been obedient with a joyful heart. In addition, use the blocks mentioned in the "visuals" section to construct a wall over time. With every act of obedience with a joyful heart, they can add a certain amount of blocks to construct the wall. A block can also be taken off for displaying unwilling, resentful obedience.

TIE IN: Recall a time in your life when God called you to a specific task. Share with your children how you responded to God's call and how you felt throughout and after the "work was complete."

PRAY TOGETHER

FOR SUCH A TIME AS THIS

ESTHER 3:5-11, AND 4:1-14.

OBJECTIVE: To help you children understand that everything happens for a reason.

VISUALS: A ball and a table. If you do not have a ball, use another object. Roll the ball across the table and let it hit the floor. Explain: The ball fell for a reason. God put gravity in place. If there was no gravity, the next time you jumped you would not come down! God allows things to happen for a reason.

WARM UP: Pray. Read 3:5-11 and 4:1-14 with your children and discuss the following:

1. Ask and explain: Have you ever had something happen in your life and thought, "I can't believe this happened to me?" Esther probably felt this way a few times. How do you think Esther felt when she was chosen to be the new queen? Esther's parents died when she was young. Her older cousin Mordecai raised her. I bet when her parents died and she was chosen to be queen, she thought, "I can't believe this happened to me."

2. Reference Esther 3:5-11. Ask and explain: Why did Haman hate Mordecai and what was Haman planning on doing to the Jewish people? Mordecai refused to bow down and worship Haman. Haman hated Mordecai and all the Jewish people. He planned to kill them all. God

knew all this would happen and that is why He allowed Esther to be chosen as queen. Esther was a Jewish person and as queen, she was in a great position to save the Jewish people from Haman's evil plan.

3. Explain how God used the events in Esther's life to shape her into the person He wanted her to be. With God, nothing happens by accident; everything happens for a reason. Mordecai advised Esther to tell the king about Haman's plot, but if anyone approached the king without being called, he could be put to death. Ask: How would you feel if you were Esther? What would you do? Mordecai gave great advice. He said to Esther, "And who knows but that you have come to royal position for such a time as this?" God had allowed her to be queen at just the right time to help save the Jewish people.

4. Explain how Esther approached the king and told him of Haman's plan. The king had Haman put to death and passed a law that saved the Jewish people. God allowed Esther to be queen for a reason: to save the Jewish people. With God, everything happens for a reason.

KEY POINT: God allows things to happen in your life for a reason. Trust Him.

APPLICATION: Tell your kids that when something happens that causes them to say, "I can't believe this happened to me," they can ask God, "What do you want to do in my life through this situation?" Encourage your children to talk through and pray about times like these as a family.

TIE IN: Share about an "I can't believe this happened to me" time. Share with your children how God used that situation to shape and mold you.

PRAY TOGETHER

THIS IS ONLY A TEST

JOB 1:7 - 2:10

OBJECTIVE: To help your children understand that God will bring tests into their lives and to encourage them to respond to those tests in a godly way.

VISUALS: As a fun test, play a game of Simon Says to test your children's listening skills. Get faster and faster each round.

WARM UP: Pray. Read Job 1:6 – 2:10 with your children and discuss the following:

1. Ask and explain: What kinds of tests have your teachers given you in school? What is the purpose of a test? A good teacher always helps you prepare for the test beforehand. God is the greatest teacher of all. He allows tests to come into your life because He is preparing you to spend eternity with Him.

2. Mention that Satan said Job only loved God because God blessed his life. Satan suggested to God that if the blessings were taken from Job, His faith would fail. Ask: How was Job's faith tested? Why can you still have faith in God through times of testing? Read Romans 8:28 with your children and explain to them that God has a purpose behind every test. Job did not understand why he was being tested, but he trusted God the whole time. Your children too can trust

God through every test because God is working everything out for their good and He will never let them be tempted or tested beyond what they can handle.

3. Encourage your children to trust God not only when times are good, but also when times are tough. Mention: God tests your obedience when your parents ask you to do something. God tests if you're following Him when the people you are with are not acting in a way that honors God. Will you follow them? What do you do when you realize the TV show you are watching is not honoring God? That also is a test of following Him. Sometimes you will be in situations wherein you are tempted to lie, steal or cheat. These are tests of honesty.

4. Illustrate how in all of Job's testing, he did not sin against God. At the end of his testing, God doubled everything Job had lost. Job did not keep his faith in God to get blessed; he kept his faith in God because God is God. Mention: The reason you should remain faithful is not so that God will bless you more, but because He is God.

KEY POINT: God allows tests to help you grow spiritually and He is always with you to help you.

APPLICATION: Throughout the day, notice the different tests that come into your life. Use each test as an opportunity to pray to God and talk about it as a family.

TIE IN: Share with your children a time when God tested you.

PRAY TOGETHER

THE GREAT SHEPHERD

PSALM 23

OBJECTIVE: To help your children understand the role of a shepherd and that God desires to shepherd them through life.

VISUALS: Any kind of rod or club (a solid stick will do); a staff with a hook on the end (a cane will do if you can get one); a stuffed animal, lamb or sheep.

WARM UP: Pray. Read Psalm 23 with your children and discuss the following:

1. Let your children hold the club and staff (cane). Ask: What do you think shepherds used these tools for? Explain to your children that the rod was used as a weapon against threatening animals. When King David was a boy watching his father's sheep, a bear and lion attacked the flock and David struck the lion and bear to rescue the sheep (I Samuel 17:34-36). The rod or club was also used to clear a path by beating bushes and branches out of the way. The staff with the hook was used to pull sheep away from danger and return them to the flock. It was used to guide the sheep in the right direction and also to pull it close to the shepherd for examination. Use the cane and stuffed animal as an illustration of gently pulling the sheep back. Sheep can be very

stubborn animals wanting to go their own way and do their own thing.

2. Explain that the shepherd lovingly cares for the sheep, protecting it from harm and making sure that it has enough to eat and drink. Ask: How is God a shepherd in your life? What does God use as His "rod and staff" to protect you and guide you? Share with your children that as a believer in Jesus Christ, God gives us His Holy Spirit to help guide and direct us in godly ways. God has also given us His Word, the Bible, to keep us from sin and protect us from being tricked by Satan's temptations.

3. Ask and explain: Verse 1 says, "I shall not be in want." What do you think King David meant when he wrote that? As you faithfully follow God, the "Great Shepherd," He will provide for you everything you need throughout your entire life. God will always be with you, and because of that, you need not be afraid.

KEY POINT: God is your Great Shepherd.

APPLICATION: Have your kids name some ways they have felt God shepherding their lives. Ask: How has He guided you? When have you sensed He was directing you in some way? Have them intentionally look for ways God is trying to shepherd them today.

TIE IN: Share with your children a specific time when you sensed God shepherding your life. How did you know it was God working in your life?

PRAY TOGETHER

TRUSTING THE SHEPHERD

PROVERBS 3:5, 6

OBJECTIVE: To encourage your children to trust God wholeheartedly.

VISUALS: Play a game of Trust-Fall. Clear a spot on the floor and have your children one at a time stand with their backs to you and their eyes closed. Position yourself behind them. On your signal, have one child at a time fall back into your arms. Catching them is important so be sure you are ready as well. The purpose of this exercise is to help your children know they can trust you even though they cannot see you. Use it as an illustration of trusting God wholeheartedly even though they cannot see Him.

WARM UP: Pray;. Read Proverbs 3:5, 6 with your children. Play Trust-Fall. Then discuss the following:

1. Ask your children how they felt falling back into your arms. What kind of thoughts were going through their minds? Did they have doubts that you would catch them? Why or why not?

2. Ask: What does it mean to "trust in the Lord with all your heart?" Help your children understand that it means to have full confidence in God's plan for them and no doubts about God's love for them. Let your children know that they can "fall back" into God's love and grace because He is always there for them.

Cross Fit FOR KIDS

3. Ask: What did Solomon mean when he said, "Lean not on your own understanding?" Ask your children some questions like God asked Job: How did God know how big to make the earth? How did God know where to put the earth in outer space? How did God make the ocean waters stop and not overflow the land? How did He put the stars in the sky? How big is the universe? These questions are not meant to make your children feel dumb. Rather they are to help them realize that God understands a lot more than they do. Help them to see that when they do not ask God for help and when they do not pray for God's will, they are living by their own understanding which will most likely lead them the wrong way. "In all your ways acknowledge Him," means to pray about everything.

KEY POINT: You can trust God wholeheartedly.

APPLICATION: Ask your children, "Why can you trust God wholeheartedly?" Listen to their responses and reassure them of God's love for them and that He has a plan for them.

TIE IN: Share with your children a time when you were in a situation and you were unsure of the outcome, but you prayed and left the results up to God. How did things turn out? Share with your children how relying on God helped your faith and trust grow.

Pray Together

THE MAIN THING

ECCLESIASTES 12:13-14

OBJECTIVE: To help your children understand that following Jesus Christ is the most fulfilling lifestyle they could ever live.

VISUALS: Bubbles that you blow with a wand.

WARM UP: Pray. Read Ecclesiastes 12:13-14 with your children and discuss the following:

1. God made a promise to Solomon that if he would live for the Lord and honor Him, then his kingship would be blessed; but if he turned away from the Lord and served other gods and did not obey His commands, then God would remove His blessing from Solomon's kingship. Unfortunately, when King Solomon grew older, he did not follow the Lord or obey His commandments like he did in his younger days.

2. Tell your children that the bubbles represent money and material possessions. As you blow bubbles, have them grab as many as possible. After they are done grabbing the bubbles, ask them what is in their hands. The answer, nothing! Their hands are empty as they will be if they are living for anything other than God.

3. Explain that Solomon tried to find happiness and fulfillment in many ways. He tried to learn as much as he could and have fun in as many ways

as he could. He tried building projects and hobbies. In all these things, King Solomon tried to fill his life with happiness apart from God. Ask: Do you think any of these things made him truly happy? King Solomon admitted all those attempts were meaningless because he was not including God in his life at that point.

4. Read Ecclesiastes 12:13 again. Explain that what King Solomon is saying is, "Now that I've tried everything, here is what I've learned: the only way to be truly happy in life is to live for God." Tell your kids: Whether you are into sports, arts, academics, whatever you set out to do, do it for the Lord. That is the main thing. Live to honor Him. That alone will bring you great joy and happiness.

KEY POINT: Make living for God the "main thing" in your life.

APPLICATION: Ask your kids to memorize Colossians 3:17 and put it into practice in all areas of their lives (chores, play, activities or school work). Ask your kids to take joy in the fact that God is honored and is smiling as they live for Him.

TIE IN: Tell your children of an instance in your life when you accomplished something or bought something with the expectation that it would make you happy, but instead it left you still wanting.

PRAY TOGETHER

A PICTURE OF LOVE

SONG OF SONGS 1:1-4

OBJECTIVE: To help your children discover the depth of God's love for them.

VISUALS: Cut out some pictures of things your children love: desserts, foods, toys, activities etc. Lay them on the table. Have your children share how they feel about the images. Tell them that the Song of Solomon is a picture of how much God loves them.

WARM UP: Pray. Read Song of Songs 1:1-6 with your children and discuss the following:

1. Mention that Solomon wrote 1,005 songs in his life, but this is the only one that God chose to put in the Bible. It is the best one he ever wrote. The Song of Songs is the story of Solomon being in love with a young woman who also loves him, and they got married. The book is also a picture of Jesus Christ's love for you. Solomon is a picture of Jesus and the young woman represents everyone who loves Jesus.

2. Express that in verse 2a, the young woman says, "Let him kiss me with the kisses of his mouth…" Mention: You can only kiss one person at a time. This represents total commitment to Jesus Christ. The enemy will try to get you to love games, movies, friends, money, etc., more than Jesus. Jesus said, "But seek first His kingdom and

His righteousness and all these things will be given to you as well" (Matthew 6:33). As you keep Jesus number one in your life, He takes care of every need you have.

3. At the end of verse 2, the woman says, "For your love is more delightful than wine." Explain that the spiritual idea is that nothing in this world compares to having a close friendship with Jesus. Proverbs 18:24 says Jesus is "a friend that sticks closer than a brother." The apostle Paul says in Romans 8 that nothing in this world can separate you from the love of God.

4. Read verse 4 and share with your children that just as this young woman loved the king and wanted to be where he was, so too, as they fall more in love with Jesus, they will want to honor Him with the way they live their lives. As they walk with the Lord, they'll want to be where He is.

KEY POINT: God is in love with you and excited about you.

APPLICATION: This week, tell your children that whenever they hear a song being played, they should stop and remind each other that God loves each of them so very much.

TIE IN: Share with your children an incident when they were infants and you held them in the middle of the night or a time when they needed comforting and you scooped them up and held them close. Reiterate how much God desires to hold them close through life.

PRAY TOGETHER

TAKING IT TO GOD

ISAIAH 37:14-20

OBJECTIVE: To guide your children to seek God in prayer when faced with difficult situations.

VISUALS: Several sheets of paper. On each sheet of paper write a struggle or potential challenge your child is facing or going to face. For example, if he is nervous about starting a new school year, write that across the paper. Maybe she is having a hard time with somebody at school. Write that person's name across another sheet of paper, and so on. These written struggles will be spread out before the Lord just as Hezekiah spread the threatening letters he received before the Lord.

WARM UP: Pray. Read Isaiah 37: 14-20 with your children and discuss the following:

1. Explain how the Assyrian army was the most powerful and feared army at this time. They were wicked and ungodly. In contrast, King Hezekiah was one of the godliest kings ever to rule in Judah.

2. Mention that the Assyrian army came to Jerusalem to destroy Hezekiah and the people of God. He sent Hezekiah threatening letters that said they were going to wipe Hezekiah and the people out. Ask: Do you think Hezekiah was scared? What do you think Hezekiah did? Read verses 14 and 15.

3. Share with your children that when they are faced with difficult situations like Hezekiah, they can take it straight to God in prayer. Let them know that they can always come to you for help, but you may not be with them during certain times, like at school. God is always with them and ready to help them.

4. Read verse 20 again with your children. Help them to see that the goal of their prayer and situation should always be to honor God.

KEY POINT: When faced with tough times, take it straight to God in prayer.

APPLICATION: Using the sheets of paper, have your children write their difficult situations and challenges down in big letters and then spread them out before the Lord and pray over them. Have the children give them to God in confidence and faith that He will help them through each and every one of those.

TIE IN: Read verses 37:35-37 so your children can see how God delivered Hezekiah. Share with your children a difficult situation you once faced. Share how you dealt with it and how God saw you through.

PRAY TOGETHER

SHAPED FOR PURPOSE

JEREMIAH 18:1-6

OBJECTIVE: To help your children see that God has created them with purpose.

VISUALS: Clay or play dough, a coffee mug, plate, bowl, saucer, etc. Display the flatware and discuss the different uses and purposes of them. If time permits, allow them to experiment with the clay or play dough by shaping vessels or items.

WARM UP: Pray. Read Jeremiah 18:1-6 with your children and discuss the following:

1. Ask and explain: Who do you think the potter represents in these verses? Who does the clay represent? God is the potter and you are the clay. What are some ways God shapes your life? God gives you specific talents and abilities to use for His purposes. God also uses life experiences, situations you go through, to teach you lessons and shape your life.

2. Ask and explain: What do you think it means that the clay was marred in the hands of the potter? The clay had imperfections, maybe air bubbles in it that caused the vessel not to be shaped correctly. What imperfections do you have? Sin. What did the potter do with the messed up piece of clay? He lovingly reshaped it to a vessel that was best for it.

3. Explain and ask: God the Father shapes you with purpose because He has a plan for your life. Hold up a piece of play dough or clay and ask, "What if this play dough or clay said, "Put me down. I'll shape myself. I don't need your help?" The clay or play dough would live its life with no purpose and it would never reach its potential. The same is true with your life. God loves you and has the best plan for your life because He knows how He made you. People get into trouble and fail to enjoy life because they are not allowing God in their lives. You will be happiest when you obey God and allow Him to use your life to bring Him glory.

KEY POINT: God has created you with purpose.

APPLICATION: Display a plate, coffee mug, bowl and pitcher. Ask: What if the plate said, "I'm tired of holding food. From now on I'm going to hold soup?" What would happen? What if the pitcher said, "I refuse to contain anymore lemonade. From now on, I will pour out peanut butter and jelly sandwiches?" How would that work out? Just as there is a specific purpose for these vessels, express that God has a purpose for their lives. Emphasize that when they are living to glorify God in their choices, attitude and actions, they are living with the purpose God created for them and they will have great joy in that.

TIE IN: Share with your children how God has shaped you, how He has gifted you. Share the kinds of talents and abilities you see in your children.

PRAY TOGETHER

FAITHFULNESS IN PURPOSE

LAMENTATIONS 3:21-26

OBJECTIVE: To help your children see that true contentment comes from a relationship with Jesus.

VISUALS: Any old toy that they used to love when it was first received. Or a family pet that they really wanted badly, but after awhile was not played with like it once was.

WARM UP: Pray. Read Lamentations 3:21-26 with your children and discuss the following:

1. Point out that Jeremiah told the Hebrew people to stop worshipping false gods. He told them to stop living sinful, wicked lives and return to the Lord wholeheartedly or God would bring judgment on them. Not only did the people not listen, but they beat Jeremiah up several times and put him in prison. Even his own family did not want to talk to him anymore.

2. What Jeremiah had prophesied for over 40 years was now taking place. The Hebrew people did not repent and turn toward the Lord so the Lord allowed the Babylonians to destroy Jerusalem and take them into captivity. Jeremiah was sitting on a hill watching the city burn as he cried for the people.

3. Read verse 24 again. Explain: Jeremiah was able to preach faithfully and walk in great obedience and love for the Lord because the Lord was his

Chapter

25

Cross Fit FOR KIDS

73

portion. Ask: What do you think it means for the Lord to be your portion? Usually portion means only a part of something, but to Jeremiah portion meant everything. Jeremiah was saying that the Lord was his portion meaning that the Lord was his everything and was most important to him.

4. Explain the following to your kids: Many times you might think, "If I can have just one more, I'll be happy," or, "If I can play a little longer, I'll be happy." You might think, "If I can just have that toy or that game, I'll be happy." What Jeremiah discovered was that true happiness is not found in things, but in a relationship with God. If you have the attitude of "just a little more" or "just one more time," you will always have a restless spirit, never really being satisfied. One of the keys to life is learning to appreciate and enjoy what God gives you and be satisfied with that.

KEY POINT: God is your portion.

APPLICATION: Use the visual here. Ask: What happened after they had the new pet for a month or two? What happened when the excitement of the new "thing" wore off? Explain that if "things" are their portion, they will never be satisfied, but if Jesus is their portion, they will be truly satisfied.

TIE IN: Share with your children a time when you fell into the "things are my portion" mentality. What did you learn from that experience that you can pass on to your children?

PRAY TOGETHER

THE FACE OF A FOLLOWER

EZEKIEL 1:4-9

OBJECTIVE: To help your children develop Christ-like character.

VISUALS: Stuffed animals and/or images of a man, a lion, an ox and an eagle. It could be pictures of just their faces or you could capture their whole bodies.

WARM UP: Pray. Read Ezekiel 1:4-9 with your children and discuss the following:

1. Mention that Ezekiel was a prophet who saw many visions. This vision was of a heavenly scene, but the four faces of the four living creatures described the character of Jesus and also the Christ-like character we should have. Each face stands for a character trait.

2. Explain that the face of a man stands for humanness. Although Jesus was the Son of God, He was also human. He got tired, hungry, and frustrated, but He never sinned. Jesus often got up early in the morning to pray to His Father. Mention: Just as Jesus needed to pray, so you need to pray all the more in your humanness. John 15:5 says, "… Apart from me, you can do nothing." Don't forget your humanness and your need for prayer.

3. Discuss how the face of a lion stands for bravery and boldness. Just as a lion is king of the jungle, Jesus is the King of Kings. Mention: Having the

face of a lion means you stand up for what you believe. As a lion, you become bolder to share your faith with others and to stand for what is right.

4.   Explore how the face of an ox stands for serving. The ox is trained for serving others, and Jesus says in Matthew 20:28, "The Son of Man did not come to be served, but to serve." Mention: If you want to be more like Jesus, have the face of an ox and serve your family, friends and others. There is no better way to let your life shine than through serving.

5.   Illustrate that the face of an eagle stands for holiness. The word holy means to be set apart, and eagles are set apart from other birds. They fly higher and farther, they do not need to fly in flocks, and they are the only birds capable of looking directly into the sun. Mention: Just as the eagle is set apart, the Word of God says you should be set apart for a lifestyle of holiness.

KEY POINT: Develop the characteristics of the four faces and you will be Christ-like.

APPLICATION: Challenge your children to work on the characteristics of these four faces. When you see them displaying the Christ-like traits say, "Great job on being an eagle!" Or, "You are really doing well at developing the spiritual lion in you."

TIE IN: Pick one of the faces and tell your children of a time you displayed that Christ-like character trait.

PRAY TOGETHER

UNDEFILED

DANIEL 1:6-9

OBJECTIVE: To challenge your children to be committed in their faith.

VISUALS: www.bible-history.com/babylonia/ and click on archeology. Also, visit www.architecture.about.com/library/bl-babylon.htm for modern shots of ancient Babylon. This will give your children a picture of where Daniel made his stand.

WARM UP: Pray. Read Daniel 1:6-9 with your children and discuss the following:

1. Explain that Daniel was getting ready to make an exciting stand. The year was 605 B.C. and King Nebuchadnezzar of Babylon came down with his army and took over Jerusalem. The finest young men of Jerusalem were captured and taken back to Babylon to be trained in the ways of the Babylonians to serve King Nebuchadnezzar. Daniel, about fifteen years old, was one of those young men.

2. Mention how the young men were assigned new names in hopes they would forget about their faith in God. The name Daniel means "God is my judge." His new name, Belteshazzar, meant "Bel protect the king." Bel was a popular false god of the Babylonians. As part of their training, they were given meat that was sacrificed to false

gods. Eating the meat meant you now worshipped the false god that the animal was sacrificed to. Most of the guys ate the meat, but Daniel refused. He made a stand for God and would not allow himself to be defiled, polluted or poisoned by the Babylonian ways.

3. Explain how ancient Babylon is like today's world. Mention the following: The world tries to tell you what kind of music to listen to, TV shows to watch, and attitudes to have in order to be popular and fit in. The world tries to influence how you treat family and others. The world's ways are not God's ways and the world's ways will leave you feeling hurt, empty and separated from God.

4. Ask and explain: How can you be more like Daniel at home, school and with your friends? How can you be sure you will not get polluted by the world's ways? Remember, God blessed Daniel greatly because Daniel made a stand for God.

KEY POINT: Honor God by making a stand and He will honor you.

APPLICATION: Ask your children to continually look for opportunities to pray out loud, help and serve others and share their faith. If they are at a friend's house and inappropriate music is being played or an inappropriate TV show is being watched or inappropriate words are being said, encourage them to use the situation as an opportunity to be a Daniel and make a stand.

TIE IN: Share with your children a time in your life when you made a stand for God. What were the circumstances? Was it difficult? How did God honor you through that?

PRAY TOGETHER

DON'T FORGET GOD

HOSEA 13:4-6

28

OBJECTIVE: To help your children pray to and worship God in times of blessing and times of trouble.

VISUALS: Display a lot of food or water bottles. I used two cases of bottled water with my children.

WARM UP: Pray. Read Hosea 13:4-9 with your children and discuss the following:

1. Start with your visual. Point out the supplies you displayed and ask, "If I gave you this pile of food or water, would you depend on me tomorrow to meet your need in that area?" Explain to your children that many times when we are blessed and our needs are met, we forget to depend upon God to further meet our needs. It is easy for us in times of blessing to forget that God is the one who constantly provides for our needs. Human nature is to call upon God in times of trouble, but to forget God in times of blessing. Throughout history, when God blessed His people, they forgot about Him.

2. Briefly highlight the story of the exodus from Egypt: God miraculously set the Israelites free through a series of plagues on the Egyptians. God supernaturally parted the Red Sea for them to cross through. God protected the people with a pillar of clouds in the day and fire by night. He

provided manna and quail for the people to eat, and water to drink. Shortly after each time God provided, the Israelites forgot about God's goodness and slipped back into the sin of complaining. God had to remove His blessing and allow the Israelites to experience hard times so they would place their faith back in Him.

3.   Mention how it is important for your kids to develop the habit of praying and worshipping God no matter what circumstances they are facing. Most people only pray during tough times and forget about God when all is going well. God wants them to pray for help during tough times, but He also wants them to remember Him in times of blessing. They remember God when they thank Him and continue to rely on Him even though all their needs may be met.

KEY POINT: Do not just seek God in the hard times, but seek Him in times of blessing too.

APPLICATION: Throughout this next week when God allows something good to happen in your children's lives, encourage them to say out loud, "Praise God." When God allows a difficult situation to come into their lives, again say out loud, "Praise God." Ask them to ask the Lord to help them through. Explain that this is a good practice because it will help them get into the habit of remembering God in good times and hard times.

TIE IN: Share with your children a time in your life when you forgot about the Lord because life was going smoothly. How did God get you to remember Him once again?

PRAY TOGETHER

MAKING UP FOR LOST TIME

JOEL 2:25

OBJECTIVE: To help your children realize that when they are disobedient to God, consequences will follow. As they repent and return to the Lord, He is able to restore lost time.

VISUALS: Any pictures of locusts you can find. One good source is www.nationalgeographic.com/animals/bugs/locust.html. Just below "Locust Profile" and "Fast Facts," click on the video: Locust Research.

WARM UP: Pray. Read Joel 2:25 with your children and discuss the following:

1. After playing the locust video from the *National Geographic* website and/or showing your children pictures of locusts, explain to them that God had been warning His people for years to turn back to Him. The Israelites fell in love with false gods and did not respond to God's warnings. They were destroying themselves through their wickedness and sin. God in His love sent the locusts to get the Israelite's attention back on Him.

2. Explain how the great swarm of locusts completely destroyed the land. Every tree, every field, every crop, every blade of grass was eaten. All the water was gone. Starvation was rampant. Sounds of weeping and wailing filled the land. God's people were left with nothing. They had no choice but

to turn back to God. Say: God will do whatever it takes to get your attention.

3. Mention that a false god or idol is anything in their lives that keeps them from passionately loving God. Some examples might be a celebrity they really like, sports, TV, music, a hobby etc. Mention there is nothing wrong with these things, but if they love things more than they love God, the things will distract them away from God. Ask: At times, are you tempted to love something more than God? Tell your kids to be careful not to make a poor choice like the Israelites made when they turned away from God to worship things.

4. Explain: If you choose to spend any part of your life loving something more than God, you will be wasting valuable days, months or years by missing opportunities in which God wants to use you. Through God's amazing grace, He is able to restore lost time and opportunities when you sincerely repent and return to Him. He did so with the Israelites.

KEY POINT: Do not waste time by falling in love with false gods.

APPLICATION: Ask your kids to check their lives. Is there anything they treasure more than their relationship with the Lord? If so, pray with them asking God to help them love Him more than the other things.

TIE IN: Share with your children a time in your life when you became side tracked from following Jesus. How did He get your attention back on Him?

PRAY TOGETHER

MEASURING UP

AMOS 7:7-8

OBJECTIVE: To help your children avoid the trap of comparing themselves to others.

VISUALS: A level. A plumb line or something similar like a piece of cord with a small weight tied to the bottom. The small weight could be a fishing weight.

WARM UP: Pray. Read Amos 7:7-8 and discuss the following with your children:

1. Share that Amos was an ordinary, common man. He was a fig farmer and sheep herder who God used as a prophet to speak to the people of Israel. Amos was used mightily because he was obedient to God.

2. Amos had a vision of God standing by a wall with a plumb line. Show your children the plumb line and share with them that it was used in construction to tell if a wall or beam was straight up and down. Demonstrate this by holding the plumb line by a corner or your wall. Show them a level which is more commonly used today.

3. Explain: God has given you a plumb line to help you follow Him and not stray off the course of following Him. His plumb line, the Bible, is absolutely true and unchanging. You might hear other people say things like, "It's okay because everyone disobeys his parents. It's okay because

my parents will never find out. That person has one so I should too. If they get to watch that TV show then I should be able to also." You cannot measure right and wrong based on what somebody else thinks or does because his wall or life is already crooked. The only true measuring tool is God's Word. Make your decisions based on what God's Word tells you and how the Holy Spirit directs you.

4. Point out that Amos was ordinary and common, yet God used Him mightily. Amos did not try to be like someone else nor did he try to change the way God made him. God used Amos the way he was because he had a faithful heart. Mention the following: Do not get caught up in comparing yourself to someone else. God loves you and will use you greatly the way you are as you continue to grow in your faith.

KEY POINT: God's Word is the true plumb line to measure your life with.

APPLICATION: Encourage your kids. Every time they are tempted to compare themselves to someone else, to thank God for who they are and ask Him to use them just the way they are.

TIE IN: Share with your children a victory in your life when you made a decision based on the plumb line of God's Word and it kept you from making a poor choice.

PRAY TOGETHER

PRIDE BEFORE THE FALL

OBADIAH VERSES 1-4

OBJECTIVE: To help your children understand what a prideful attitude is and how God feels about a prideful attitude.

VISUALS: When you get to number two, show your children pictures of the rock city of Petra where the Edomites lived. You can do a Google search on Petra or visit www.grisel.net/petra.htm.

WARM UP: Pray. Read Obadiah 1-4 with your children and discuss the following:

1. Share with your children that Edomites were descendants of Esau. Esau had a twin brother named Jacob and the two fought each other from the time they were in the womb. God changed Jacob's name to Israel and from his family came the Israelite people. Meanwhile, Esau grew rebellious toward God and mean spirited toward his brother. The Edomites came from Esau.

2. As years passed, Esau's descendants always fought with the Israelites – Jacob's descendants. The Edomites would never help the Israelites fight against their enemies, but rather they rejoiced over the Israelites being defeated. The Edomites became very prideful. They built an incredible rock city called Petra in which they carved all the buildings and houses right in the mountains.

Show them pictures of Petra on the website. The Edomites believed that no one could conquer them and they felt they did not need God anymore.

3. Explain to your children that an attitude of pride expresses a desire to live apart from God. When people are prideful, they do not think they need God's help in their lives. God allowed Petra to be totally destroyed because the Edomites were so prideful. Pride always leads to a fall.

4. Ask and explain: How do you know you are getting prideful? There are two major ways. First, you no longer pray like you used to. Prayer is a dependence upon God to help you through life. Pride says, "I don't need God. I'll live my own life." Second, you are no longer as thankful as you once were. All good things come from the Lord and you should thank God for everything. When you have pride in your life, you think everything good that happens is because of you and you no longer have a thankful heart towards God.

KEY POINT: Pride always leads to a fall.

APPLICATION: Invite your children to kneel and pray with you. Have them ask God if they have been prideful. If the Lord reveals pride in their lives, agree with God that it is sin and ask Him to help them have a humble spirit. This week focus on praying more and being thankful in all things. Parents help your children develop a deeper prayer life by increasing the frequency with which you pray.

TIE IN: Share with your children a time when pride caused a fall in your life. How did God restore you?

PRAY TOGETHER

RUNNING FROM GOD

JONAH 1:1-5

OBJECTIVE: To show your children that running from God is never a good idea.

VISUALS: Weights (these could be dumbbells or something as simple as a medium to large book).

WARM UP: Pray. Read Jonah 1:1-5 with your children and discuss the following:

1. Point out that God said, "Go," and Jonah said, "No." God wanted Jonah to go to Nineveh and tell the Assyrians about God. Jonah did not like the Assyrians because they were a very mean and cruel people. The Assyrians would put hooks in people's mouths and lead them away into slavery and they tortured people in very brutal ways. Jonah did not want to go because the Assyrians might believe in God and receive His mercy and forgiveness.

2. Explain: God asks you to be obedient too. For example, His Word instructs you to obey your parents, pray for your enemies, love people (including your siblings), not to lie and not to steal etc. In verse 2, we read that Jonah paid money to get on a ship that was heading in the opposite direction from where God wanted him to go. Sin will always cost you something. Ask: What are some ways that sin is costly to you?

3. Ask: Why was Jonah in the bottom of the boat sleeping? He was exhausted from running away from God. Use the **visual** by having your children hold the weight (book or other item) with their arms out straight for as long as possible. Explain to them that holding the weights in this way represents disobedience to God in this analogy. As they tire and their arms give way, ask them how it feels and let them know that disobedience to God will be exhausting to them spiritually, emotionally and mentally.

4. Explain: To get Jonah's attention, God caused a great storm to rage on the sea. Who else had to go through that dreadful storm? (The sailors.) Mention: Your sin never affects just you, but it affects everyone around you as well.

KEY POINT: Sin always costs you something.

APPLICATION: Explain that sometimes knowing what God wants you to do can be difficult. That is why knowing the Word of God is so important. If they know and follow the Word, they can be sure that they are in God's will. The Word of God instructs them to obey their parents, love those who harm them, share their stuff with others and tell people that Jesus loves them. Ask your kids to pick one of these instructions (obey, love, share, tell) and do it more this week than they ever have before. Encourage them to build that habit of obedience in their lives. Ask your children daily about their progress and continue to be a source of encouragement to them.

TIE IN: Share with your children either a time when you ran from God and "paid the fare," or when you were obedient to God.

PRAY TOGETHER

WHAT DOES GOD WANT?

MICAH 6:6-8

OBJECTIVE: To help your children understand what God wants from them.

VISUALS: (To be used in the application section.) If you have two or more children, have them act out short scenes of acting justly, loving mercy and walking humbly. If you have one child, play charades with him or her acting out the three things God desires from his or her life.

WARM UP: Pray. Read Micah 6:6-8 with your children and discuss the following:

1. Provide your children with some background information. God's people were not in a right relationship with God. They continually worshipped and offered sacrifices to false gods. Micah prophesied judgment on the people. In frustration the people asked, "What does God want from us?" The people should have already known what God desired of them because He told them many times in the Scriptures.

2. Explain: Micah reminded the people what God desired of them. Mention the following: God desires the same from you. First, "To act justly." To act justly means to do what is right. For example, always tell the truth, obey your parents, love people, stick up for others being picked on,

do not cheat or steal. God loves it when you do what is right because it shows you love Him. As you honor God by doing what is right, He honors you right back.

3. Explain: Second, Micah says, "To love mercy." Mercy is caring enough about another person to make a difference in his life. Have compassion on others. Feel what they are feeling and help them out. Mention: God has shown you incredible love and mercy and now He wants you to do likewise. Do not be quick to judge others. Instead, be quick to show them mercy.

4. Describe: Thirdly, Micah says, "To walk humbly with your God." Mention: Humility means understanding that everything you are (all your talents, abilities and gifts) and everything you have comes from God. Humility is not thinking of yourself more highly than you ought. The opposite of humility is pride. Pride expresses itself through an attitude of thinking you're better than those around you. Pride causes you to look down on others and live independently from God, forgetting how much you need Him in your life. Walk humbly with God.

KEY POINT: God wants you to act justly, love mercy and walk humbly.

APPLICATION: Reference the visual section. Your children can act alone or together. Encourage them to be creative.

TIE IN: Share with your children a time in your life when you acted justly, displayed mercy or walked humbly with God. What were the circumstances that surrounded that event?

PRAY TOGETHER

WHAT DO OTHERS SAY?

NAHUM 3:18,19

OBJECTIVE: To encourage your children to live a lifestyle that points others to Christ.

VISUALS: Salted pretzels and water to drink.

WARM UP: Pray. Read Nahum 3:18,19 with your children and discuss the following:

1. Give your children the following background information. Nahum is the sequel to Jonah. One hundred and fifty years earlier, Jonah had prophesied God's destruction on Nineveh, but since the people of Nineveh repented, God relented. In Nahum's day, the people of Nineveh were back to their evil ways, so God brought about their destruction. When others heard about the destruction of the Ninevites, they clapped their hands and rejoiced. Ask: What do you want others to say when they hear about you?

2. Read Matthew 5:13 to your children. Mention: You ought to care about what others think when they hear your name because Jesus wants you to be salt. Salt sprinkled on food makes the food taste better. Salt increases the flavor. Jesus wants you to be flavorful to others. Others should feel comfortable hanging around you.

3. Mention: Salt also creates thirst. If you've ever eaten popcorn, pretzels or potato chips you know

that salt makes you thirsty. Hopefully when others look at your life and the joy you have in Christ they too will become thirsty for Jesus.

4. Explain: Last, salt acts as a preservative slowing down corruption. Many times corruption comes in the form of reckless rumors and hurtful words towards others. As salt, Jesus calls us to be different and stay away from such corruption. Instead of talking negatively about others, concentrate on only saying encouraging words that build others up. Let your words be seasoned with the salt of the Word.

KEY POINT: Being spiritually salty points others to Jesus.

APPLICATION: Use the visual at this point. Give each child a salted pretzel. Have them take a few bites as you remind them of the three characteristics of salt: enhances flavor, creates thirst and hinders corruption. Briefly discuss again how they can be salt at their school, on their teams, at their activities and in their homes.

TIE IN: Share with your children a time in your life when God used you to be salt.

PRAY TOGETHER

TIME IN THE TOWER

HABAKKUK 2:1-4

OBJECTIVE: To help your children see their need to spend time alone with God.

VISUALS: In the application section, your children will build a fort/tower out of couch cushions, pillows, etc.

WARM UP: Pray. Read Habakkuk 2:1-4 with your children and discuss the following:

1. Explain: The prophet Habakkuk did not understand why God was going to use the Babylonians, a wicked group of people, to judge Judah, God's people. Ask: Have you ever gotten angry at your mom or dad because you thought her or his decision was not fair? Habakkuk did not think it was fair of God to use the Babylonians to judge Judah.

2. Explain: Habakkuk, in his anger, did not walk away from God, but instead, he went to God in a very special way. He climbed up into a rampart (tower) all by himself and talked with and prayed to God to get understanding. Mention: It would be like you turning off the TV, video games, or computer and not playing with your friends for a few hours because you wanted to be alone with God, seeking understanding and building your relationship with Him.

3. Explain: Habakkuk separated himself from the

world to get understanding from God. God told Habakkuk to write down what he learned. Mention: It is a good idea to write down or mark in your Bible the things God teaches you. Doing so will help you remember.

4. Say: God told Habakkuk, "…The righteous will live by his faith" (verse 4). You may not always understand all that God is doing in your life or why things happen the way they do. That is okay. God wants you to trust in Him and live by faith. You build your faith in God by spending time alone in the "tower" praying to God. Your tower can be your room or a special place where it is quiet and you can pray and talk with God.

KEY POINT: To grow in your faith, spend time in the tower.

APPLICATION: Give your children five minutes or less to build a tower/ fort out of couch cushions and pillows etc. Allow them to go in it. Reiterate to them that just as Habakkuk separated himself from all distractions by going in the tower to spend time with God, they need to do the same thing as well. Talk about what could be their "tower."

TIE IN: Share with your children the need in your own life as a parent to spend time in the tower. Tell them where your "tower" is.

PRAY TOGETHER

A SPIRITUAL CHECK UP

ZEPHANIAH 1:4-6

OBJECTIVE: To share with your children the importance of having spiritual checkups in their lives.

VISUALS: Any examination equipment a doctor would use even if the tools are fake (toys). For example, stethoscope, thermometer, ear scope, tongue stick, reflex hammer, etc.

WARM UP: Pray. Read Zephaniah 1:4-6 with your children and discuss the following:

1. Use your visuals to perform a mock physical checkup on your children. Ask: Why is it important to have regular physical checkups? (To see if your body is healthy physically.)

2. Explain how Zephaniah was speaking to God's people who were not very healthy spiritually. Mention that just like we need physical checkups, we need spiritual checkups as well. God's people failed to have regular spiritual checkups, and as a result wound up being very sick spiritually.

3. Point out that in each of the three verses, Zephaniah tells of the sickness with which the people were infected. In verse 4, the spiritual leaders (priests) became pagan. They began to worship Satan. In verse 5 are those who said they worshipped God, but also worshipped other false gods like the stars. Verse 6 tells of those who once

followed God, but grew far apart because they stopped praying and seeking Him. Over time, they no longer believed.

4. Mention that these three groups of people, who at one point had faith, now were far away from God because they failed to have regular spiritual checkups. Ask and explain: What is a spiritual checkup? It is time you spend alone with God to ask Him if there is anything in your life that is not pleasing to Him. Is there any unconfessed sin in your life? You should also ask God if there is anything about your life that you need to change. Allow God to answer those questions and then obediently make the changes.

KEY POINT: Staying close to God requires regular spiritual checkups.

APPLICATION: Read Psalm 139:23,24 with your children. Lead them in a spiritual checkup. Encourage them to get on their knees and have them ask God, "Search me and know my heart. Test me. Is there anything in my life that is not pleasing to you? Is there anything in my life that I need to change?" If your children feel comfortable sharing what God put on their hearts, give them an opportunity to share. Try and do spiritual checkups weekly.

TIE IN: Share with your children the importance of spiritual checkups in your own life.

PRAY TOGETHER

NOW IS THE TIME

HAGGAI 1:2-6

OBJECTIVE: To share with your children the importance of avoiding procrastination when the Lord gives them something to do.

VISUALS: Container with water in it, a glass, and a pan to catch the water overflow.

WARM UP: Pray. Read Haggai 1:2-6 with your children and discuss the following:

1. Explain how King Cyrus of Persia allowed the Jews to go back to Jerusalem and rebuild the temple (the house of the Lord) that King Nebuchadnezzar destroyed. They started working right away, but they became distracted by arguing amongst themselves. They also got discouraged by mean people living in the land. They stopped working on God's house instead building their own houses for sixteen years.

2. Ask: Have you ever heard of the Nike slogan, "Just Do It?" That was Haggai's message to the people. The people knew God wanted them to rebuild the temple; they just wanted to do it later. Haggai challenged them to just do it. Build the temple. Be obedient to God now!

3. Ask and explain: Have you ever put off your chores? You know you have been asked to clean your room, take out the trash, pull the weeds,

straighten up the garage, help with the dishes, etc., but you thought I'll do it later. That is procrastination. It is hard to enjoy life when you put off things you know you ought to do.

4. Mention: The same is true in your relationship with God. When God wants you to do something, do it right away. (Use the visual.) The glass represents your life and the water represents God speaking to you. Procrastinating with what God wants you to do is like this: Place the glass in the pan and begin to pour water into the glass until it overflows. When you don't stop and listen to God, you make a mess of your life spiritually. Things begin to pile up and then overflow when you procrastinate.

KEY POINT: Be obedient now.

APPLICATION: Have your children ask God if there is anything that He has asked them to do that they have not yet done. After a few moments, ask your children what God revealed to them. Encourage your children to complete the work. Let them know that God loves them.

TIE IN: Share an instance in your life when you knew God was asking you to do something and you procrastinated. How did you feel during that time? How did you feel once you were obedient?

PRAY TOGETHER

ROBED IN RIGHTEOUSNESS

ZECHARIAH 3:1-5

OBJECTIVE: To help your children discover their position in Christ.

VISUALS: Dirty clothes that look like rags, and a set of nice clothes.

WARM UP: Pray. Read Zechariah 3:1-5 with your children and discuss the following:

1. Explain how Haggai and Zechariah were ministering to God's people at the same time. They were both trying to motivate the people to build the temple. During the first year, the people completed the foundation, but because of arguing from within and intimidation from without, the people walked away from God's work.

2. Explain how the temple was left unfinished for sixteen years and no doubt weeds were growing up on the foundation. Joshua was the high priest in charge of spiritually leading the people. He failed to keep them on track. Ask: How do you think Joshua felt as a leader?

3. Mention how in Zechariah's vision, Joshua was standing before Jesus and Satan stood at Joshua's right side to accuse him. Satan probably brought up the fact that Joshua did not motivate the people to finish the temple and that he was a failure in leadership. Mention: The Bible says

that Satan accuses you day and night before God. Satan is always trying to tell God about your sin and all that you do wrong.

4. Mention that God answered Satan's accusations against Joshua in two ways. First, He rebuked him. A rebuke is to strongly correct someone. God defended Joshua because Joshua had faith in God. Second, God took away Joshua's old, filthy clothes which represented his sin and put brand new, rich garments on him, symbolizing forgiveness. Joshua's faith positioned him in Christ and he was forgiven.

KEY POINT: In Christ, you are robed in righteousness.

APPLICATION: Use the materials listed in the visual section. Dress one of your children in rags representing sin. The raggy clothes and nice clothes can be worn over the top of what they already have on. You play the role of Satan accusing them of sin and wrong doing. Switch roles and play the Father. Rebuke Satan and take off the rags and replacing them with "rich garments" representing forgiveness. Remind your children that because they are positioned in Christ, they are forgiven and God robes them in righteousness.

TIE IN: Share with your children something from your past that Satan tries to get you to feel guilty about. Share how God does not see your failure but rather your faith and He has robed you in righteousness. The same is true for your children's lives.

PRAY TOGETHER

BRING YOUR WHOLE HEART

MALACHI 3:8-10

OBJECTIVE: To help your children understand the blessing of tithing.

VISUALS: Ten items of anything (dollar bills, books, pencils, fruit, etc.).

WARM UP: Pray. Read Malachi 3:8-10 with your children and discuss the following:

1. Mention that when Malachi was preaching to the people, their hearts were far from God. One of the ways God knew the people were not following Him fully was that they no longer gave back to the Lord the whole tithe.

2. Explain to your children that tithe means tenth: to give one tenth of everything you earn back to God. Use the visual to demonstrate the proportion of the tithe. Ask and explain: Why do you think God wants you to give a tenth of everything you earn back to Him? Money can be powerful. The more you have, the more you want, and if you're not careful you will start thinking about money more and more. That is called greed. You think you have money, but money winds up having you.

3. Express how in Matthew 6:21, Jesus says, "Where your treasure is, there your heart will be also." Mention the following: If your treasure

is in possessions and things, that is where your heart will be, and your life will center on those things. God knows that if your treasure is in things, it will leave you feeling empty and unsatisfied. If your treasure is in heaven, your thoughts, actions and life will center on Him. Tithing helps your treasure to be in heaven.

4. Explain that God promises to "throw open the floodgates of heaven and pour out so much blessing that you will not have room enough for it" (verse 10). Mention: God wants you to give because He wants to bless you. When you bring the whole ten percent, it is like bringing your whole heart to God and He really loves that.

KEY POINT: "Where your treasure is, there your heart will be also" (Matthew 6:21).

APPLICATION: Explain how Malachi 3:10 is the only place in the Bible where God says, "Test me." Ask your kids to give faithfully to the Lord and see what He will do. I was sharing this with my kids while eating at the Cracker Barrel restaurant when our waitress brought us a bag from the Cracker Barrel store. She explained that someone in the restaurant wanted our family to have what was in the bag – it was filled with toys from the Cracker Barrel store. Mention: God is very creative in the way He gives back to you. The next time you are in church, make it a point to bring your whole tithe to God. Do this regularly and get ready to be blessed.

TIE IN: Share with your children a story from your life when God provided for you because you were faithful to bring the whole tithe into the storehouse.

PRAY TOGETHER

MAKING JUDGMENTS

MATTHEW 7: 1, 2

OBJECTIVE: To help your children discover the right and wrong way to judge.

40

VISUALS: Tape measure. A referee's shirt/and or hat if you have one.

WARM UP: Pray. Read Matthew 7:1,2 with your children and discuss the following:

1. Ask and explain: What does it mean to judge a person? In the context of verse 1, judging means to criticize or make a mean-hearted decision about a person. If you have ever used the following words or thought them in your head about someone, you have judged them: stupid, idiot, dumb, dork, etc. If you have become cold, short, and rude or are ignoring someone, you have judged them. Parents, you can ask for or give examples if you like.

2. Mention and ask: There are two types of judgment: 1. Worldly judgment that points the finger at others with the purpose of tearing people down. 2. Godly judgment that caringly and lovingly confronts another with the goal of bringing that person to Christ or restoring their relationship with Lord. Which type of judgment do you think we talked about in number 1? (Worldly.) Is worldly judgment right or wrong? (Wrong.)

3. Ask and explain: What do you think it means

when the Bible says, "With the measure you use, it will be measured to you?" You may use that old saying, "What comes around, goes around." As often as you judge others, and with the same degree of harshness that you judge others, you will be judged. Use your measuring tape as a visual. Stretch it out several feet and point harshly at one of your kids in worldly judgment. Stress that the same measure they judge will be measured back to them.

KEY POINT: We are instructed to caringly and lovingly use godly judgment with people.

APPLICATION: Use a referee and an umpire as an example. (Wear your referee shirt if you have one.) Explain that a referee judges whether you are in bounds or out of bounds. An umpire judges whether someone is safe or out. Explain to your kids that in life we've got to make judgments about what is godly and what is not so that we can stay within the bounds of God's loving protection and within the safety of His Word. Doing so helps us better follow Jesus. Explain these examples: If a friend is listening to music that's not appropriate, or looking at things on the TV or computer that you know are wrong, or using bad language, or making fun of somebody else etc., etc., it's okay to use godly judgment to quietly and gracefully help that person. If he or she doesn't respond to you, then separate yourself from this person and that situation.

TIE IN: Share a story from your life of when you either used worldly judgment or godly judgment with someone, or perhaps when either of those judgments was used on you. What were the circumstances and how did it make you feel? Have your kids share as well.

PRAY TOGETHER

TAKE CARE OF YOUR ROOTS

MARK 11: 20, 21

OBJECTIVE: To help your children see the need for taking care of their spiritual root system.

41

VISUALS: A dead tree, bush or plant and a healthy tree, bush or plant.

WARM UP: Pray. Read Mark 11: 20,21 with your kids and discuss the following:

1. Show your kids the dead tree, bush or plant. Ask them to give some reasons as to why it could have died. Read verse 20 again. Help your kids understand that when a plant gets sick or weak, it often begins with the root system.

2. Ask your kids what the purpose of the root system is. Help your kids understand that the main purpose of a root system is to anchor the tree or plant in the ground and to provide water and nutrients for growth. Ask: Is it important to take care of the root system? Why? Compare the healthy tree or plant with the dead one.

3. Mention: Just as trees and plants have root systems, you have a spiritual root system. As your spiritual root system grows, God will use you more and more to influence this world for Him.

4. Ask and explain: What will happen to you spiritually if you do not take care of your root system? Let them know that God has a plan for their lives

and that in order to live that plan out, they need to hear from God. The more they take care of their root system, the easier it is to hear God and the more clearly they will sense Him leading and the more fruitful their life will be.

KEY POINT: Take time to develop your spiritual root system.

APPLICATION: Ask: How can you take care of your spiritual root system? Help them to see that by doing this devotion they are taking care of their root system. Other ways include: prayer, worship, Scripture memory, church etc.

TIE IN: Tell your children about your spiritual root system, when you've been strong and times when you've been weak. How did you feel during those times? Describe a time in which you heard from God because you were taking care of your spiritual root system.

PRAY TOGETHER

No Excuses

Luke 14:16-24

OBJECTIVE: To help your children understand their need for Jesus.

VISUALS: A blindfold, a couple of coins and a display of food.

WARM UP: Pray. Read Luke 14:16-24 with your children and discuss the following:

1. Ask: Who is the man that prepared the banquet and invited the guests? (God.) What does the banquet represent? (A relationship with Jesus and heaven.)

2. Explain how people started making excuses as to why they could not accept the man's invitation. Ask: What was the first person's excuse? (He had just bought a field.) Why was that not a good excuse? (It was foolish to buy a field without first looking at it and it would have been too dark in the evening to see it anyway.) The field represents material possessions: stuff that can become more important to your kids than Jesus if they let it.

3. Ask and explain: What was the second person's excuse? (He had bought five yoke of oxen and he had to go test them.) Why was that a bad excuse? (One would not buy a bike without first trying it out.) The oxen represent work and play. Mention: Sometimes you can get so caught up in work or

distracted by play that you allow those things to become more important than Jesus.

4. Ask and explain: What was the third person's excuse? (I just got married.) Mention: Relationships or friends can also distract you from following Jesus. It is important to choose friends who love the Lord as much as you do.

5. After the people who made excuses did not come, the man invited the poor, crippled, blind and lame. Ask and explain: Why did the man do that? He wanted his house to be full just like God wants heaven to be full. Also, the people who were crippled and blind knew they needed help. That is why they accepted the invitation.

KEY POINT: You need Jesus because sin has crippled you spiritually.

APPLICATION: Blindfold one child and ask him or her to go get something and bring it back to you. Give the coins to another child and have him or her attempt to buy some food from you, but he or she doesn't have enough. Have one child try to open a bottle or jar with one hand behind his or her back. After trying alone, help them accomplish the tasks.

TIE IN: Explain to your children that just as they needed you to help them accomplish the tasks, we all need Jesus' forgiveness because sin has crippled us spiritually and He makes us whole through forgiveness. Do not let any excuses come between you and Jesus.

PRAY TOGETHER

HAPPY ARE THOSE WHO SERVE

Chapter

43

JOHN 13: 1-7

OBJECTIVE: To help your children discover the joy of serving.

VISUALS: A bowl of water, wash cloth and a towel to wash and dry your children's feet.

WARM UP: Pray. Read John 13:1-17 with your children and discuss the following:

1. Start today's devotion by washing your children's feet. While you wash their feet, explain to them that in Jesus' day, everyone wore sandals and walked to places they were going. All the roads were dirt so their feet would get very dusty or even muddy if it rained. By the front door of each house was a wash basin and as a guest entered a house, a servant would wash his feet so the house would not get dirty. Foot washing was a very lowly job.

2. Explain how the disciples were eating the Last Supper. It was the last meal they would have with Jesus before He went to the cross. There was no servant to wash the disciple's feet and none of them humbled themselves to do the task. As the meal was being served, Jesus got up and became their servant. He washed their feet. Ask: Why did Jesus wash the disciples' feet? (verse 15).

3. Express how Jesus saw that the disciples' feet were dirty. He did not lecture them about dirty feet or

Cross Fit FOR KIDS

talk to them about the importance of staying clean. When He saw a need, He did something about it. Mention: If you want to be like Jesus, put your faith in action and look for ways to serve others.

4. Ask and explain: What do you think Jesus meant when He said, "Now that you know these things, you will be blessed if you do them?" (verse 17). "Blessed" here means happy. True happiness in your life will come when you are serving another in the name of Christ.

KEY POINT: Happiness comes in serving others.

APPLICATION: Mention the following: Jesus doesn't want you just to remember what He has done. Nor does He want you only to talk about what He has done. He wants you to follow His example as a servant leader and do what He has done. What are some ways you can serve others at your school? On your team? In your home? Choose one or two ways you just mentioned and do them today. Come back and talk about it as family when you are done.

TIE IN: Tell your children of a time when you "washed someone's feet" by serving them. What did you do and how did you feel?

PRAY TOGETHER

UNFOLDING THE PLAN

ACTS 9:1-6

OBJECTIVE: To help your children understand why God does not reveal His whole plan for their lives all at once.

VISUALS: Make a very long "to do" list for your children. Include chores to do, tests to study for, homework, places to go, etc. Make the list overwhelming to them.

WARM UP: Pray. Read Acts 9:1-6 with your children and discuss the following:

1. Mention how Saul was a religious man. He believed in God, but did not have a relationship with God. He did not believe that Jesus was God's Son who came to save us from our sin. Saul was on his way to Damascus to put Christians in prison for their faith when he met Jesus.

2. Explain: The first thing Jesus asked Saul was, "Why do you persecute me?" Persecute means to hurt. Ask and explain: How was Saul hurting Jesus? When you do unkind things or say unkind words to family members and others, you are persecuting Jesus also. Jesus died for the person you are being unkind to and if that person is a Christian, Jesus lives in them.

3. Mention the following: Jesus told Saul to "get up and go into the city, and you will be told what you must do." God changed Saul's name to Paul. Paul

wrote two-thirds of the New Testament, started up many churches, led many people to Jesus, but he was also stoned, whipped, beaten, imprisoned, shipwrecked and eventually beheaded for his faith. What if God had told Paul the whole plan all at once? Paul would have been overwhelmed and may not have done anything! God unfolds His plan for your life in steps so you won't get overwhelmed.

4. Explain: A second reason why God unfolds His plan for your life step by step is so that you will keep going to Him for direction and help. Read Matthew 7:7,8 to your children. In the Greek, this means keep on asking, keep on seeking and keep on knocking. God wants you to continually go to Him because He wants to have a relationship with you. If God told you His plan all at once you would not seek Him nearly as much.

KEY POINT: God unfolds His plan for your life in steps.

APPLICATION: Read aloud your "to do" list from the visual section. Ask: How does hearing the whole list all at once make you feel? Explain: God, in His mercy and love, only unfolds His plan for your life in steps so you won't get overwhelmed. When you want to know the next step you have to keep asking, seeking and knocking. This helps you stay close to God.

TIE IN: Think back on a time in your life when God unfolded His plan one step at a time. Describe the situation to your children.

PRAY TOGETHER

MOLD YOUR MIND

ROMANS 12:1-2

OBJECTIVE: To help your children distinguish between living for the Lord and conforming to the world.

VISUALS: Jell-O molds, cookie cutters, cake or cupcake pans, ice cube trays, water and different shaped containers to pour it into, a piece of wood, rock or brick.

WARM UP: Pray. Read Romans 12:1-2 with your children and discuss the following:

1. Using your visuals, explain to your children that each mold is like the world in which they live. The Jell-O they put in the Jell-O mold will take that shape. The cookies will take the shape of the cookie cutter mold. The cupcakes will come out looking like cupcakes in that mold. Explain: Just like water is shaped by containers, the world tries to shape you.

2. Mention: The world has molds that try to shape your thoughts, attitudes and actions. What are some molds of this world? Some examples may include: "The comparison mold." People tend to base whether they feel good or bad about them-selves on how they compare to another person instead of basing their feelings on their relation-ship with Jesus. The "reaction mold:" If you hit me, I'll hit you. If you talk mean to me, I'll talk mean to you. The "They're doing it" mold: My

friend is disobedient to her parents so I can be disobedient to mine. Or the kids at school use that language so I can too. There are jealousy molds, lying molds, stealing molds, etc., etc.

3. Explain how Romans 12:2 says, "Do not conform any longer to the pattern (or molds) of this world, but be transformed by the renewing of your mind." Using your visuals again, explain to your children that the Word of God is like a solid rock foundation. (Use your piece of wood or rock to illustrate the solidness of God's Word.) This solid piece of material cannot be squeezed into one of these Jell-O molds. Mention: God wants you to be solid in the Word so you won't be squeezed into a worldly mold. You get rid of worldly patterns by renewing your mind with the truths of God's Word.

KEY POINT: Be careful not to be squeezed into a worldly mold.

APPLICATION: Ask your kids to pay attention as they go about their day and week, using what they learned about judging in the Matthew 7:1-2 devotional. Have them watch their classmates and friends and see if they can pick up on worldly molds. Tell them to remember not to judge for condemnation, but for identification. Encourage them not to be squeezed into those worldly molds.

TIE IN: Share about a time in your life when you found yourself squeezed into a worldly mold. What was it and how did you get out?

PRAY TOGETHER

RUNNING THE RACE

I CORINTHIANS 9:24-27

OBJECTIVE: To help your children understand what the Christian race is and how to train for it.

VISUALS: I took my children to our local track. After racing down a straightaway, we sat on the track for the devotional. I also used some leaves as an example of what the ancient athletes won as a prize.

WARM UP: Pray. Read I Corinthians 9:24-27 with your children and discuss the following:

1. Tell your kids about a race you ran sometime in your life – even if it was just at recess with your friends. Have them tell about a race experience.

2. Explain how in these verses, Paul is comparing running a race with the Christian life. Who are the runners Paul is referring to? Help your kids understand that when people place their faith in Jesus as Savior and Lord, they become runners in the Christian race to which Paul refers.

3. Ask and explain: Runners in a race compete against one another, but who are you running against in the Christian race Paul discusses? Help your kids understand that they are not competing against other Christians by doing more good works, or going to church, praying or reading their Bible more often than others do. They are actually running against themselves, challenging

themselves to do those good works to become more like Jesus. That is the Christian race: to become more like Jesus Christ every day.

4. In a physical race, name some ways runners train. Ask and explain: How do you train for your Christian race? It is by doing things that help you have a strong relationship with Jesus and to fall deeper in love with Him. For instance, having devotions, hiding God's Word in your heart by memorizing Scripture, worshipping, developing your prayer life – all of these actions train your heart to be more in line with Jesus' plan for your life.

KEY POINT: In the Christian race, your goal is to be more like Jesus every day.

APPLICATION: Ask your kids to put their training exercises to work and name some people who they can have a positive influence on. Who can they encourage at school? What can they do to help their teacher? How about cleaning their room without being asked or helping around the house more? Mention that there are many ways to become more like Christ and He will bless them for it.

TIE IN: Share with your children an example of something you did in your Christian race that blessed somebody else and drew you nearer to God.

PRAY TOGETHER

CHOOSE YOUR YOKE WISELY

II Corinthians 6:14-16

OBJECTIVE: To help your children understand what "being yoked together" means and why God does not want believers and unbelievers yoked together.

VISUALS: Go to Google images and type in "oxen yokes" to give your children a visual of yokes. In the application section, play a game of opposites. Have your children try to move forward and backward at the same time, up and down at the same time. Have them pat their heads with one hand and rub their stomachs at the same time with the other. Although they may be able to do that, it takes much thought and is not natural.

WARM UP: Pray. Read II Corinthians 6:14-16 with your children and discuss the following:

1. Explain that a yoke was a piece of farming equipment used to join two or more oxen together to plow a field. Deuteronomy 22:10 says, "Do not plow with an ox and a donkey yoked together." Ask your children why they think God's Word says this.

2. Mention how in today's verses, Paul gives a list of opposites: righteousness and wickedness, light and darkness, Christ and Belial (ancient name for Satan), believer and unbeliever, and the temple of God and idols. Mention: Just like these things cannot have harmony together, neither will

you have peace and joy in a relationship that is unequally yoked.

3. Mention: Paul is not saying that you should not talk to or play with anyone who is an unbeliever, but rather this is a warning to be very careful with whom you become close friends with and with whom you spend much of your time. Most of your "hang out" time should be spent with believers. It is important not to have an attitude that because you love the Lord, you think you are better than others; but it is just as important that you guard yourself carefully in your selection of close friends because your life will be influenced greatly by those you hang around most.

4. Explain: God is not trying to control your relationships, but rather He is trying to protect you from harm and heart-ache. Just like Paul's list of opposites cannot have harmony together, God knows that ultimately a relationship with an unbeliever can only go so far before there is pain and disappointment.

KEY POINT: Do not be yoked together with unbelievers.

APPLICATION: Use the visuals as an example of being unequally yoked.

TIE IN: Share with your children a time in your life when you were unequally yoked relationally or professionally. What was the result?

PRAY TOGETHER

SOWING WISELY

GALATIANS 6:7 AND 9

OBJECTIVE: To give your children a good understanding of the spiritual principle of sowing and reaping.

VISUALS: Seeds of any kind to illustrate sowing and reaping.

WARM UP: Pray. Read Galatians 6:7 with your children and discuss the following:

1. Explain to your children that sowing and reaping are farming terms used to describe planting and harvesting. (Mention: Whatever seeds you sow or plant are what you will reap or harvest in return. Use the seeds as a visual. If you sow orange seeds you will reap oranges. The same is true with your life. Whatever a person sows in life is what he will reap.)

2. Have your children name some kinds of attitudes and actions that people sow in life and what they reap from those attitudes and actions. For example, when a person sows honesty, he reaps trust. When a person sows responsibility by cleaning up her mess, ask your children what she would reap. When a person sows hatred, he gets hatred in return.

3. Ask your children to explain what they think God's Word means when it says, "Do not be deceived: God cannot be mocked" concerning the law of reaping and sowing. (Do not be tricked!

Your actions and words will come back to you. You can't get around this law. It applies to everyone.)

4. Ask: What does it mean to sow God's Word? (It means living out God's Word by being generous with others, sharing, helping, praying, praising God, telling others about Jesus, being honest, showing kindness, etc. Mention: When you live your life like this, you are sowing seeds of God's love to others. Verse 9 tells you when you sow spiritual seeds like these, you may not see what you reap until you get to heaven, but keep sowing those good seeds because they sprout up and make a huge difference.)

KEY POINT: Sow wisely because what you sow is what you will reap.

APPLICATION: Ask your children what are some areas of their lives that they would like to do a better job of sowing into. Ask them to make a short list of these and keep them in their Bible. Tell them to take a look at their list often and pray that God will help them sow wisely in those areas of their lives.

TIE IN: Share with your children a time in your life when you reaped what you sowed, whether it was a positive or negative experience. What did God teach you?

PRAY TOGETHER

FIGHTING THE RIGHT BATTLES WITH THE RIGHT ARMOR

EPHESIANS 6:10-18

OBJECTIVE: To help your children fight the right battles with the right armor.

VISUALS: Pictures of or actual examples of weapons and armor.

WARM UP: Pray. Read Ephesians 6:10-18 with your children and discuss the following:

1. Ask them why someone would need to wear armor. Help them understand that they are in a spiritual battle and there is spiritual armor for that battle.

2. Ask them what they think Paul meant when he wrote, "Our struggle is not against flesh and blood... but against the spiritual forces of evil in the heavenly realms." (Flesh and blood mean other people who can be seen. Your battle is never against others, but Satan, who is unseen. He is causing arguments, bickering and fights to take place. Don't give in to Him. Be wise.)

3. Mention: Instead of fighting your battles with ugly words or angry hands, Paul gives you a suit of armor to wear that is effective for fighting spiritual battles and standing against Satan's schemes.

- **The Belt of Truth:** that your life would be buckled tightly with honesty and godly character knowing the truth of God's Word.

- **The Breastplate of Righteousness:** as you walk in a right relationship with the Lord, your heart would be pure and protected from evil and wickedness.

- **Feet Fitted with the Readiness that Comes from the Gospel of Peace:** that you are not walking over people, but quick to be a peacemaker.

- **Shield of Faith:** your faith in Christ is what strengthens you to stand firm and protects you from the enemy's schemes when Satan comes at you.

- **The Helmet of Salvation:** remembering it is by God's grace that you are saved and by His grace He will protect your mind in the battle.

- **Sword of the Spirit:** the only offensive weapon mentioned. The enemy cannot stand against the Word of God for it is powerful and effective. Use it.

KEY POINT: Fight the right battles with the right weapons.

APPLICATION: Use your visuals and stress to your children how ineffective these weapons are in fighting Satan. Read Ephesians 6:18 again. Prayer is how the battles are won!

TIE IN: Share with your children a time in your life when you either fought the right battle in the right way or when you fought the spiritual battle in a physical way. What was the result?

PRAY TOGETHER

BEING CONTENT

PHILIPPIANS 4:11-13

OBJECTIVE: To help your children understand that true happiness and contentment only come through a relationship with Jesus Christ.

VISUALS: A square peg and a round hole or any visual like that. A hardcover book into a plastic cup or try putting your foot in their shoe. Illustrate that no matter how hard you try to cram certain things in defined spaces, they will not fit.

WARM UP: Pray. Read Philippians 4:11-13 with your children and discuss the following:

1. Ask them what the word "content" means. (It means to have enough, to be satisfied, to be filled. Many people think content means to get what they want. For example, I'll be happy when I get a puppy. Or, if I can just have that toy or video game, I'll be happy. The problem is when the excitement of that "new thing" wears off they will want something else and that cycle will never end until they realize where to find true contentment.)

2. Explain that Paul said he learned to be content whether he had a lot or a little. Ask your children what they think Paul's secret of being content was. (Paul learned that material things and money just left him wanting more and more. Knowing

that he was going to heaven, a place where "stuff" does not matter, his contentment was now based on his relationship with Jesus and living for Him.)

3. Mention that Pascal, a mathematician and philosopher who lived a long time ago, said, "Every person was created with a god-shaped void in them that can only be filled with God." Ask: What do you think he meant by that? Explain that every person, including each of your children, has a hole in his or her soul that can only be filled with Jesus. Tell them: Remember, "stuff" will not make or keep you happy. It will just make you want more and more.

4. Ask your children if they have ever said, "Can I have just a little more?" Or, "Can I do it one more time?" (Be careful! There will always be more and there will always be another time. Learn to enjoy what you have been given and you will be content.)

KEY POINT: True contentment is found in Jesus Christ.

APPLICATION: Illustrate the visual with your children. Try to fit and cram objects into spaces that they will not fit into. Explain to your children that they have a hole in their souls that can only be filled with Jesus. Cramming "stuff" into their lives will only leave them wanting more, leading them to be unsatisfied and restless their entire lives.

TIE IN: Share with your children a circumstance in your life when you were satisfied with whatever God had for you.

PRAY TOGETHER

FULFILLING YOUR PURPOSE

COLOSSIANS 1:15,16

OBJECTIVE: To help your children see that fulfilling their life's purpose is directly linked to living for God.

VISUALS: Tools and/or utensils. For example, a hammer, screwdriver and pliers. Or a fork, spatula and ladle.

WARM UP: Pray. Read Colossians 1:15, 16 with your children and discuss the following:

1. Explain to your children that the "firstborn over all creation" refers to Jesus Christ, but it does not mean God created Him first. Jesus always existed as He and God are one. "Firstborn" means that Jesus is greater, higher and ruler over all things created.

2. Ask your children, according to what Paul says in verse 16, how many things were created by God. (All things. That means you are a creation of God. Not only that, but why did God create you?) Reread the last sentence of verse 16. (You were created for God.)

3. Mention that many people think God exists for them. They try to make deals with God saying, "God, I promise I'll be good if you allow me to have that toy or pet, etc." Or, "God, I promise I'll study harder next time if you let me get a good grade on my test." God does not exist to

make you happy. Rather, you exist to bring God pleasure.
That is your purpose.

4. Read Ephesians 2:10 to your children. The word "workman-
ship" literally means masterpiece. Explain the following:
You are God's masterpiece. His fingerprints are on you.
God created you with talents and abilities to do good works
for Him in this world. That is His plan for your life. As you
allow God to rule and have first place in your life, He shows
you His plan and helps you use your talents and abilities for
His glory.

KEY POINT: You were created by God, for God.

APPLICATION: Use your visuals to illustrate that each item has a purpose.
Demonstrate that purpose. Ask your children what would
happen if the screwdriver said, "I want to be a hammer?" Or if
the ladle said, "I want to be a spatula." Would they be effective
in fulfilling their purposes? Share with your children some gifts,
talents and abilities you see in their lives and how they might
use them for God.

TIE IN: Ask your children how they think God has gifted them. Share
with them how you feel when you are using your God-given
talents to serve God and others.

PRAY TOGETHER

MARKERS FOR MATURITY

I THESSALONIANS 5:15-18

OBJECTIVE: To help your children mature spiritually by seeing specific, spiritual markers to work on.

VISUALS: Treasure hunt. Make three or four clues in which each clue leads to the next. The third clue leads them to the treasure where a Bible is hidden. This can be done inside or outside. The clues that build up to the treasure represent markers for spiritual maturity. This will be done in the application section.

WARM UP: Pray. Read I Thessalonians 5:15-18 with your children and discuss the following:

1. Explain that spiritually, their goal is to grow to be more Christ-like. Mention the following: Paul gave you some markers like clues to help you reach that goal. Reread verse 15 for the first marker. It is a great mark of maturity when people wrong you and instead of getting back at them you are kind to them and forgive them.

2. Explain that a second marker for maturity is to "be joyful always." Mention that their joy should not depend on good or bad things happening in their lives, but rather help them see that God is using all those things to expand them in their relationship with Him and to prepare them for heaven. God causes all things to work for their good. In that they can be joyful.

3. A third marker for maturity is, "Pray continually." Mention the following: No matter where you are or what you are doing, you can talk to God. You can pray as you are walking, playing or even taking a test. God wants to be in a conversation with you throughout your whole day.

4. A fourth marker for maturity is, "Give thanks in all circumstances." Mention the following: As you love the Lord, He will not let anything happen in your life unless He allows it. Therefore, those things that do happen in your life, God has a plan and a purpose for. You can be thankful for that.

KEY POINT: Markers for maturity will help you be Christ-like.

APPLICATION: Use the Treasure Hunt exercise from the visual. After completing it, ask your children what the goal was. (To find the treasure.) Ask them, "What helped you reach the goal?" (Clues along the way. Those clues are like markers that brought you closer to the goal. In the same way, the spiritual markers that Paul gave you today will help you grow to spiritual maturity.)

TIE IN: Choose one of the four spiritual markers and share with your children a situation from your life in which you applied that marker.

PRAY TOGETHER

DOING RIGHT

II THESSALONIANS 3:13

OBJECTIVE: To help your children never tire of doing what is right in God's sight.

VISUALS: Bible, couch or chair.

WARM UP: Pray. Read II Thessalonians 3:13 with your children and discuss the following:

1. Ask your children to try and guess why the Thessalonians were getting tired of "doing what is right." False teachers were lying to them by saying Jesus already came back to take believers to heaven. As a result, the Thessalonians lost their hope in the Lord and they became tired and lazy in their faith.

2. Ask this: Would you get tired and lazy in your faith if you thought Jesus had already come back and you were not taken to heaven? Why or why not? How would you live differently if you really believed Jesus was coming back for you today?

3. Explain that Paul gave the Thessalonians three specific things that he did not want them to grow tired of: 1. Standing firm in the Word of God (2:15). Don't be wishy-washy in your faith. Live by God's Word no matter where you are and who you are with. 2. Praying. "Finally, brothers, pray…" (3:1). No matter where you are or what's going on in your life, pray. 3. Being productive

for the Kingdom (3:10-11). These people stopped using their talents and abilities for God. They became idle like a parked car – ineffective for the Kingdom. Explain how living with an expectation that Jesus will come back at any moment will help your kids stand firm in the truth of God's Word. It will help them pray about everything and focus on using their gifts and talents to glorify God.

KEY POINT: Live your life expecting Jesus to return at any moment.

APPLICATION: Have your children stand on one foot with their eyes closed. Push them slightly to get them off balance. Explain to them that that position represents not standing firm in the Word. A lack of prayer will cause them to be off balance in life and unproductive for God. Next, have your children kneel on their Bibles in a prayerful position with their elbows resting on a chair or couch. The foundation they are kneeling on is the Word of God. The object they are leaning against is Christ and they are in a position of prayer. Try to knock them off balance and explain to them that living with an expectancy of Christ's return helps them stand firm, remain prayerful and be productive. They will be much steadier in life while living with the expectancy of Jesus' return.

TIE IN: Share with your children how your life would change if you really believed Jesus was coming back today. As a family, commit to live in this way.

PRAY TOGETHER

SHIPWRECKED

I TIMOTHY 1:18-20

OBJECTIVE: To help your children understand what a spiritual shipwreck is so they can steer clear of one.

VISUALS: If you have access to the internet, go to www.opacity. us/gallery87wrecks.htm. Or show them a map of where many shipwrecks have occurred at www.shipwreckcentral.com and click on shipwreck map. If you do not have access to the internet, try to locate a magazine photo of a shipwreck.

WARM UP: Pray. Read I Timothy 1:18-20 with your children and discuss the following:

1. After looking at photos of shipwrecks, ask your children why they think shipwrecks happen. Ask the following: What do you think is happening on board the ship during a shipwreck?

2. Ask your children to name some of the consequences of being shipwrecked. You may mention loss of life, loss of cargo, injuries, emotional trauma for survivors, etc.

3. Paul mentions that Hymenaeus and Alexander have shipwrecked their faith. Ask: What do you think shipwrecked faith looks like? Apparently these two men sincerely believed in Jesus at first, but then they started blaspheming. What do you think that means? (Let them know that blas-

pheming is spreading lies and wrong ideas about faith in Jesus.) As a result, they led a lot of people astray.

4. Ask: What is the difference between sinning and ship-wrecking your faith? Explain to your children that when they sin, the right thing to do is confess it to God and ask forgiveness from who they sinned against. That keeps their fellowship with God strong. Shipwrecking one's faith means they know they are sinning and are unwilling to stop. Instead, they go deeper and deeper into sin without turning back to God or asking for forgiveness. That person is no longer living under the protection and blessing of God.

KEY POINT: "Holding on to faith and a good conscience" will always steer you clear of shipwrecking your faith.

APPLICATION: Explain that true faith is loving God with all your heart, soul, mind and strength and a good conscience is confessing sin as it occurs while asking for forgiveness when needed. Ask your kids to take some time right now to ask God if there is any sin in their lives that they need to tell Him about and if there is anybody they need to go and ask forgiveness from.

TIE IN: Share with your children a time when God was leading you to ask for forgiveness from somebody. How did you respond? How did it make you feel?

PRAY TOGETHER

STAYING FOCUSED

II TIMOTHY 2:3-7

OBJECTIVE: To help your children be victorious in their walk with the Lord.

VISUALS: A picture or figurine of the following: soldier, athlete and farmer.

WARM UP: Pray. Read II Timothy 2:3-7 with your children and discuss the following:

1. Show them the visual of the soldier. Explain to your children that soldiers have specific orders or commands given by their commanding officers that they must follow to give the military the best chance of victory. What would happen if soldiers became distracted and ignored those orders and commands? Jesus is your commanding officer and His Word is like a set of commands to help you have victory in life. The enemy, Satan, wants to distract you from God's Word.

2. Show them the visual of the athlete. Explain that athletes have rules to follow for competing. If an athlete ignores the rules by taking steroids or disregarding team curfews and policies, he will be disqualified from competition and the prize. Share with your children that Jesus is their Head Coach in life. The Bible is His set of guidelines to protect them against being disqualified for the prize – loss of reward in heaven.

3. Show them the visual of the farmer. Explain that farmers must be hard-working to harvest crops. The opposite of hard-working is lazy and careless. What would happen to a farmer's field if he became lazy and careless with the seed he planted? (The good seed would be overtaken by weeds and bugs would begin to destroy the crop.) Ask: What would happen to you spiritually if you became lazy and careless with your prayer life and devotions?

KEY POINT: Spiritual victory takes diligence.

APPLICATION: Use recent news to find examples of soldiers, athletes and spiritual leaders who are at the top of their professions without having to compromise good character. Also, show examples of soldiers, athletes and spiritual leaders who became distracted and disqualified because of poor choices. Encourage your children to stay focused spiritually by praying and having devotions regularly.

TIE IN: Share with your children a time in your life when you were either lazy or diligent in your walk with the Lord.

PRAY TOGETHER

CHANGED BY GRACE

Titus 2: 11-13

OBJECTIVE: To help your children be motivated by grace in their relationship with God.

VISUALS: To be used in the application section. Use the following analogy to discuss motivation for obedience with your children. If I said, "I command you to clean your room," would you do it? If I said, "I will reward you with money if you clean your room," would you do it? If I said, "As one who loves and cares for you and provides all that you need in life, I want you to clean your room," would you do it? Which way of getting you to clean your room is correct? (They are all correct. As the parent you have the right to command, reward and ask for obedience.) Which is the purest and most desired response of obedience? (Obedience out of an understanding of your gracious provision.)

1. Ask and explain: What do you think grace is? Grace is forgiveness you receive from God even though you did not deserve or earn it. Grace is also receiving blessings from God that you cannot earn and you don't deserve. It is because of God's grace that you are going to heaven even though your sin deserves hell.

2. Explain that when the children read verses 11 and 12 together, they learn that grace teaches them to say no to sin. Ask: How do you think grace

teaches you to say no to ungodliness and sin? (Explain to your children that when they understand how good God is to them and realize that He freely gave His Son to die on the cross so they can be forgiven, it should cause them to want to love, obey and serve God forever.)

3. Reread verse 13. Ask: How will waiting for the Lord's return help you live a godly life? Explain to your children that waiting for the Lord is not like sitting in a chair staring out the window waiting for their friend to come by. Mention the following: Waiting for the Lord means you are living your life as if Jesus were coming back today. Would you watch the same TV shows? How would you treat your brothers and sisters? Parents?

4. Express the following: Understanding the depth of God's grace and realizing that Jesus can come back at any moment should cause you to live a holy, pure life.

KEY POINT: God's grace is your motivation for obedience.

APPLICATION: Challenge your children with the analogy of motivation found in the visual section.

TIE IN: Share different stages of your spiritual life in which you responded to God with the three different motivations for obedience: command, reward, grace.

PRAY TOGETHER

CHARGE THAT TO ME

PHILEMON 11 AND 18,19

OBJECTIVE: To help your children understand that Jesus willingly took their sin and charged it to Himself.

VISUALS: Pencil or pen, small pieces of scrap paper, a cross. If you do not have a cross, you may be able to make a simple one out of two small twigs or pieces of wood.

WARM UP: Pray. Read Philemon 11 and 18,19 with your children and discuss the following:

1. Share with your children Philemon's story. Philemon was led to Christ by Paul. Philemon had a slave named Onesimus who stole from him and ran away to Rome. While Onesimus was in Rome, he met Paul and Paul led him also to Christ. As a new Christian, Onesimus was helpful to Paul. Onesimus' name means useful or helpful.

2. Explain that according to Paul, before Onesimus became a Christian, he was useless to Philemon; but when he turned his life over to Jesus, he became useful. Ask: Why was Onesimus now useful to Philemon like his name suggested? (Because as a follower of Christ, Onesimus would now be trustworthy, hard working and a brother in faith.)

3. Ask your kids the following: Paul knew the right thing to do was to send Onesimus back

to Philemon, but would Philemon forgive Onesimus for stealing and running away? What would you do? With regard to Onesimus' sin, Paul told Philemon to "charge it to me." What do you think that meant? (Paul would pay back the money Onesimus took even though Philemon owed Paul his life because Paul led him to Jesus.) Philemon knew that Jesus paid for his sin so he should forgive Onesimus' sin.

4. Mention the following: You are made useful for God's Kingdom because Jesus willingly took your sin upon Himself on the cross. John 15:5 says, "Apart from God, you can do nothing." Apart from faith in God, you can do nothing that pleases God or is useful to Him.

KEY POINT: Jesus charged your sin to Himself.

APPLICATION: Have your children write down some of the sins they have committed, those things they know have hurt God. Then have them fold the paper and pin or tape it to the cross to symbolize Jesus charging their sin to Himself on the cross. Reiterate that because of the cross, they are forgiven and made useful.

TIE IN: Share with your children a time when you were forgiven by someone or you freely forgave someone who sinned against you.

PRAY TOGETHER

RUNNING A GREAT RACE

HEBREWS 12:1, 2

OBJECTIVE: To help your children understand how to run a great spiritual race.

VISUALS: Any of the following: rope or anything to tie ankles together, blindfold, weights, things that would tempt your children to go off course.

WARM UP: Pray. Read Hebrews 12:1,2 with your children and discuss the following:

1. Ask your children what they think the race is that is mentioned in these verses. Help them see that their race is to follow Jesus. It is to become more like Him every day. In this spiritual race, ask them who they are running against… Explain that it is not against other believers or even Satan. Your goal is to be more like Jesus, so you are actually running against yourself.

2. Ask your children: How does Satan try to hinder and entangle you in the race? What does perseverance mean? Webster's defines perseverance as "To persist in or hold to a course, belief etc. in spite of obstacles." Why do you think you will need perseverance to run your spiritual race?

3. Ask what your children think "the race marked out for us" means. Explain that the goal of the race is the same for every believer to become more Christ-like. But the race course is different

for each believer because God gives people different gifts, talents, abilities and personalities. Mention the following: It is very important not to compare yourself with other believers in the race because their race is not the same as yours. Comparing yourself to others may leave you feeling bad or defeated because you think the other person is running a better race. Or comparing yourself could lead you to thinking of yourself more highly than you should. That is not Christ-like.

4. Ask and explain: How can you avoid being hindered by Satan or entangled by sin? "Fix your eyes on Jesus." How can you fix your eyes on someone you cannot see? By faith, when you read the Word, pray and worship you are fixing your eyes on Jesus. You will become most like what fix your eyes on.

KEY POINT: Your race is to be more like Jesus.

APPLICATION: Use your house as an obstacle course which represents the spiritual race. Tie ankles and/or use a blindfold to hinder and entangle your children from finishing the race. Use items (favorite toys or games) to entice them to come off course. Explain that this is often Satan's strategy to hinder them from being like Christ. Stress to them not to compete or compare with one another. Untie them and remove the distractions. Have them focus on your instructions through the course to symbolize "throwing off everything that hinders and entangles."

TIE IN: Share a time in your spiritual race that you almost got pulled off course.

PRAY TOGETHER

SANITIZING YOUR SPEECH

JAMES 3:5-10

OBJECTIVE: To help your children be aware of the dangers that reckless words can cause.

VISUALS: A match or lighter and a piece of paper.

WARM UP: Pray. Read James 3:3-10 with your children and discuss the following:

1. Light a match or use a lighter to show your children the small flame it produces. Transfer the flame to a piece of paper and watch it grow. (You may want to do this outside or over your sink.) Explain to your children that although the flame is small, once it gets out of control it can burn down the house and cause huge amounts of damage and irreplaceable loss. Mention: Though your tongue is small compared to the rest of your body, when you lose control of it, it will cause much damage.

2. Read Proverbs 12:18 to your children: "Reckless words pierce like a sword, but the tongue of the wise brings healing." Explain that you cannot control what others say to you or about you, but every day you have control over your words and whether they are reckless or wise. Reckless words destroy lives while wise words heal hearts. Which do you want to use?

3. "Sticks and stones may break my bones, but

names will never hurt me." Why is this saying not true? Bones heal, but names (words) penetrate your heart and soul and they hurt very much. Some studies show that it takes nine positive comments to cancel out one negative.

4. Mention that in Psalm 19:14, David prayed, "May the words of my mouth and the meditation of my heart be pleasing in your sight..." Ask: How does your heart impact your words? Explain to your children that what they think about and meditate on in their hearts will come out of their mouths. The more they worship, pray and take in God's word, the wiser their words will be to others.

KEY POINT: Wise words bring healing.

APPLICATION: Have them memorize Proverbs 12:18, "Reckless words pierce like a sword, but the tongue of the wise brings healing." Ask them to encourage at least two people every day and talk about it as a family at night.

TIE IN: Share with your children an experience in which you were either encouraged or discouraged greatly by another. How did it affect you?

PRAY TOGETHER

PREPARING FOR ACTION

I Peter 1:13-16

OBJECTIVE: To help your children understand that their life in Christ should be action oriented.

VISUALS: To be used in the application section: a stack of several books, one being a Bible.

WARM UP: Pray. Read I Peter 1:13-16 with your children and discuss the following:

1. Ask and explain the following to your kids: Before you run a race, play a sport or take a test, do you think about what you are about to do? What goes on in your mind? Thinking about the race, game or test before you partake in it helps prepare your mind and gets you ready to do it. Peter says, "Prepare your minds for action; be self–controlled, set your hope… in Jesus." Peter wants you to be ready to serve the Lord, be kind to others and say no to sin. Your life in Christ is action all the way.

2. Read verse 14 again. Ask and explain: What are evil desires? (Your sin nature wanting you to be disobedient to God and parents. It's knowing what is right, but doing what is wrong.) Peter explains that you may have acted that way before you knew Jesus, but now that you know Jesus, your actions should reflect your relationship with Him.

3. Explain that holy means to be set apart for God. There are
    two parts to being holy. The first is God makes you holy
    when you trust in Jesus. In Christ you are made holy, pure,
    forgiven. The second part of being holy has to do with how
    you are living. This is a day to day process of becoming
    more and more like Christ. This process will continue your
    entire life. You will fail at times, but God even uses your
    failures to bring about holiness in you. As you rely on God
    to give you strength and courage, He will help you live a
    holy life, different and set apart for Him.

KEY POINT: My life in Christ is action oriented, leading to holiness.

APPLICATION: Use your visual. Display a stack of books of which one
is a Bible. Pull the Bible out of the stack and set it alone.
Explain that the Bible is made up of sixty-six different books
and written by forty different authors over a time period of
fifteen hundred years. The Bible was written on three different
continents in three different languages. The Bible is holy, set
apart and different. Explain that your children too are called to
be holy. Encourage and hold each other accountable for living
holy in your thoughts and actions.

TIE IN: Share with your children how your desire for holiness has
changed your decision making.

PRAY TOGETHER

NOTHING LACKING

II PETER 1:3-8

OBJECTIVE: To help your children see that God has given them everything they need to live a godly life.

VISUALS: To be used in the application section: a mixing bowl and a simple recipe. For example: pancake mix and water, or waffle mix, eggs, oil and water. You may want to use a simple cookie recipe. A Bible.

WARM UP: Pray. Read II Peter 1:3-8 with your children and discuss the following:

1. Repeat to your children, "His divine power has given us everything we need for life and godliness..." What do you think Peter meant by "has given?" Explain to your children the verb is past tense, meaning that God has already put in them everything they need to live a godly life. There is nothing they still lack to be godly.

2. Explain that verses 5-8 contain a list of ingredients that God has put in your children. Goodness – desire to please God, knowledge – understanding of God, self-control – submitting yourself to God's will, perseverance – to keep your faith no matter what is happening around you, godliness – living as Jesus would, kindness – consideration of others, love – deeply caring for others. Ask your children which of these ingredients they see most in themselves and in each other.

3. Mention that in verse 5, Peter says, "Make every effort to add to your faith…" Lay a closed Bible in front of your children and ask them if the Word of God is powerful. It is powerful, but only if they use it. That is what Peter meant when he said, "Make every effort." Explain: The ingredients Peter listed to live a godly life are already in you, but if you do not put them into practice, how will you be able to live out your faith in Christ?

KEY POINT: God has already given you everything you need to be godly.

APPLICATION: Have the ingredients from the visual displayed before your children and tell them what they can make if they use all the ingredients. If they do not use the ingredients, they will never be all that they can be. If they never add the ingredients Peter mentions to their faith, they will be ineffective and unproductive spiritually.

TIE IN: Choose one of the ingredients from the text and share with your children how God used that quality in you.

PRAY TOGETHER

LAYING DOWN YOUR LIFE

I JOHN 3:16-18

OBJECTIVE: To help your children discover what living out their faith should look like.

VISUALS: To be used in number four. On three separate sheets of paper, write out each of the following dilemmas. On the first sheet: A friend comes over and you really want to go outside and play, but your friend wants to stay inside and play video games. On the second sheet: You brought your two favorite snacks to school to eat with your lunch. You hear a classmate say he is still hungry, but he has no more food. On the third sheet: You love the activity you are playing at recess, but notice one of your classmates is left out. Optional: If you have more than three children you can make up additional dilemmas.

WARM UP: Pray. Read I John 3:16-18 with your children and discuss the following:

1. Explain that a true Christian is a follower of Christ. Mention the following: Just as Jesus laid down His life for you, you are challenged to lay your life down for others. What does it mean to lay down your life? You no longer think of yourself as being the most important, but instead are sensitive to the needs of others and are interested in serving them as an example of Jesus.

2. Ask: Have you ever noticed someone in need?

What was the situation? Read verse 17 again. What does John say about having pity (mercy) on someone in need?

3. Read verse 18 again. Ask and explain: When it comes to exercising your faith, what is the difference between using words and taking action? Saying words is like telling your friends about chocolate cake. Taking action is baking a chocolate cake and giving some to your friends. Which is more powerful? Which would Jesus do?

4. Have your children pick a dilemma, read it out loud and respond to it.

KEY POINT: Living out your faith takes action.

APPLICATION: Ask each of your kids to look for at least one person every day in whom they can lay down their lives (as described in number one), have mercy on or take action with. Have them report back to your family regarding what happened. Encourage them to exercise their faith in the same way each day so it becomes a living habit.

TIE IN: Share with your children a real life dilemma you faced in which you laid down your life, showed mercy or put your faith to action. What happened?

PRAY TOGETHER

TRUTH AND LOVE

II JOHN 1-3

BJECTIVE: To teach your children the balance between truth
and love.

63

VISUALS: To be used in the application section. A rope or belt
– anything that can be used for tug of war. If you have
a park nearby with a seesaw, that would be a good
visual as well.

WARM UP: Pray. Read II John 1-3 with your children and
discuss the following:

1. Share with your children some background
   information on John. John had a brother named
   James who was also an apostle. James was the first
   apostle martyred while John was the only apostle
   not martyred. These brothers were called the
   "sons of thunder" because they had hot tempers.
   In Luke 9: 51-56, John and James asked Jesus if
   they could call fire down from heaven to destroy
   a Samaritan town. Jesus rebuked them for their
   lack of love towards people.
2. Explain that even though love did not come
   naturally to John, he later became known as
   the disciple of love. John talked about love and
   encouraged believers to love each other more
   than any other Bible writer. Ask your kids: What
   do you think made this dramatic change in John's
   life?

3. Mention that love is genuinely caring for and having compassion on another person. Along with love, John also spoke truth. Truth is correcting others for their own good. There is a balance necessary when using truth and love. Ask your kids to picture a seesaw (or better yet, show them one if you have access to one). Ask them: If the seesaw is unbalanced with too much love on one side or not enough truth on the other, what would happen? (A good illustration is offered when you, the parent, sit on one end of the seesaw and have your child sit on the other to demonstrate the lack of balance.)

4. Explain and ask the following: Sharing truth without love will leave a person feeling hurt, discouraged and sad. Sharing love without truth allows the other person to continue on in behavior that is harmful and hurtful. How would you feel if I was always telling you what you were doing wrong in a harsh way? What if I never corrected you?

KEY POINT: Truth needs to be shared in a loving way.

APPLICATION: Use the rope or belt in a match of tug of war. One person is truth and the other love. Instruct the love side to barely pull. Ask: What happens? Do the same with truth. Pull equally on both sides. The rope is tight. Mention the importance of remembering the tension and balance between truth and love that needs to be there when talking with others.

TIE IN: Share with your children an instance in your life in which too much truth was shared without enough love. How did it make you feel?

PRAY TOGETHER

BUILDING YOUR REPUTATION

III JOHN

OBJECTIVE: To help your children care about the reputation they are building.

VISUALS: Pictures of animals. For example, a lion, shark, snake, dog, rabbit and horse.

WARM UP: Pray. Read III John with your children and discuss the following:

1. Ask your children what a reputation is. If they need help defining it, explain that a reputation is how a person views another. For example, former President Abraham Lincoln had a reputation for being kind. Jesus had a reputation for healing people.

2. Show your children the visuals and ask them what the reputation of each animal is.

3. Mention how Gaius, Diotrephes and Demetrius were three men John mentioned in his letter. Ask and explain: What was the reputation of each man? Gaius had a reputation of being faithful, trustworthy and welcoming. Diotrephes had a reputation of loving to be first which means he wanted to be in charge of everything – bossy. He also talked badly about others. Demetrius had a reputation of being well liked by everyone who knew him, and his life lined up with the truth of

God's Word. Demetrius did not just talk about the Word of God; he lived it.

4. These men built their reputations little by little every day by the way they acted and treated others. Explain and ask: Every day you are building a reputation too. Which one of these three men do you want to be like most and why?

KEY POINT: Every day you are building your reputation.

APPLICATION: Hold up the visuals again. Ask: If this was your picture, what would others say your reputation is? (They don't have to answer out loud, but have them think about it.) Have your children close their eyes. Ask them, "What about your reputation do you want God to help you change?"

TIE IN: Share with your children how God has changed your reputation since you became His follower.

PRAY TOGETHER

Know What You Believe

JUDE 1-4

OBJECTIVE: To help your children have a clear understanding of what they should believe.

VISUALS: To be used in the application section: a box of cake mix, or anything similar. Your driver's license.

WARM UP: Pray. Read Jude 1-4 with your children and discuss the following:

1. Explain that Jude wrote to warn the early Christians about false teachers spreading lies in the church. The first lie was regarding, "Godless men, who changed the grace of our God into a license for immorality" (verse 4). Hold up your driver's license. Ask and explain: What does this give me the freedom to do? Just like my license gives me freedom to drive, godless men were teaching that Christians have a license or freedom to sin because they were under God's grace. How do you feel about that?

2. Mention that the second lie was, "Godless men, deny Jesus Christ our only Sovereign and Lord" (verse 4). Explain that this is the lie of heresy. Heresy has to do with adding to or taking away from the grace of God. It is heresy to believe that you need to add to what Jesus did on the cross by doing good works to earn forgiveness. It is also heresy to believe that Jesus Christ is not the Son

of God who died for your sins and the sins of the world. That is taking away from what the Bible teaches.

3. These lies were and still are being taught. Mention that it is important to know what the Bible teaches about forgiveness and salvation so that your kids know what to believe.

- Everyone is sinful. Read Romans 3:23.
- Sin leads to a spiritual death called hell. Read Romans 6:23.
- Salvation is a gift of God that cannot be earned by man. Read Ephesians 2:8,9.
- Forgiveness of sin and salvation comes from faith in Jesus Christ alone. Read Acts 16:31.

KEY POINT: Jesus Christ is the one true God. Believe in Him.

APPLICATION: Use your ingredients. You do not have to actually open things up and mix them together, but you can use your imagination. Add silly things to the recipe like a picture, ball and a book, etc. Ask: Would this still make cake? No! Take away some ingredients from the recipe. Ask: Would this still make cake? No! Mention that God has given us the recipe for being a Christian found in the bullet points above.

TIE IN: If your children have never placed their faith and trust in Jesus and they want to now, lead them in prayer, saying: **Lord Jesus, I believe that you are the Son of God. Thank you for dying on the cross for me. Right now, by faith, I place my trust in you for the forgiveness of my sins. Thank you for your grace in my life. Help me to follow you all of my life. Amen.**

PRAY TOGETHER

RED HOT FOR JESUS

REVELATION 3:14-20

OBJECTIVE: To help your children be red hot for Jesus.

VISUALS: To be used in the application section: an ice cold drink that your children love, a hot drink that either you or your children love, and a lukewarm drink. If you prefer, you can use the analogy of ice to put on a bruise which keeps swelling down, a heating pad to loosen sore muscles and lukewarm water.

WARM UP: Pray. Read Revelation 3:14-20 with your children and discuss the following:

1. Explain that revelation was written by John, the last, living apostle around 95 A.D. After failing to kill him by boiling him in oil, Domitian, the new Roman Caesar, banished John to the Island of Patmos. Revelation literally means uncovering the truth. Chapters 2 and 3 were messages from Jesus to seven churches that John ministered to. John wrote down the message and sent them to the churches. Today's devotion focuses on Jesus' message to the seventh church, Laodicea.

2. Mention that Hieropolis, known for its hot water springs, was a city close to Laodicea. The two cities partnered together to build an under-water aqueduct to pipe the boiling hot water to Laodicea. The problem was that by the time the water reached Laodicea, it was no longer hot,

but lukewarm. Jesus compared the Laodicean's faith to the lukewarm water. Tell your kids that if you are hot for Jesus, meaning you love Him with all your heart, mind and strength, He can use you. If you are cold for Jesus, not desiring to live for Him, He can deal with you. However, being in a lukewarm state is dangerous because it means you are numb and desensitized to Jesus. Being lukewarm, you do not see your need for Jesus.

3. Illustrate how the Laodiceans had a lot of money, nice clothes and good medicines. They seemed to have it all, but Jesus described them as "wretched, pitiful, poor, blind and naked." Ask and explain: Why did He describe them in this way? The people were poor spiritually, blind to the truth of God's Word and pitifully lukewarm in their faith. Real wealth is living your life to honor God. That shows you love God, and by doing so, He stores up treasures in heaven for you.

KEY POINT: Be red hot for Jesus.

APPLICATION: Use your visuals to show your children that there is little use or desire for lukewarm water. Just as lukewarm water is gross, living lukewarm for the Lord is sickening to Jesus. Ask and explain: What are some ways you can demonstrate you are red hot for Jesus? Be obedient to what He is leading you to do, sharing your faith, showing kindness, etc.

TIE IN: Share with your children a time in your life when you felt you were slipping into lukewarm living. What caused it? How did God bring you out of it?

PRAY TOGETHER

CONCLUSION

Congratulations to your entire family. Finishing this devotional took determination, perseverance and a great desire to want to know God better. Great job! As a parent, you helped establish a firm spiritual foundation for your child; and as a child, I'm sure both your love for and desire to live for Jesus has increased. Continue living out your faith.

As a family, where do you go from here? When my kids and I finished CROSS✝FIT, we definitely wanted to build on the habit of spending time in the Word. The following are some things we've done as a family to keep CROSS✝FIT:

- We've studied the parables of Jesus.
- We've gone through the book of Proverbs.
- The kids are now beginning to lead family devotions every other week.
- In addition, you can start CROSS✝FIT FOR KIDS again and make your way from Genesis to Revelation a second time.

The sooner you and I as parents can teach our children to grow spiritually on their own and depend on the Holy Spirit, the more mature they will be.

Again, congratulations, and may you and your family continue on the journey.

To order additional copies of CROSS†FIT
or CROSS†FIT FOR KIDS please visit

www.jasonanthony.net